PORTRAIT OF HAMPSHIRE

Portrait of
HAMPSHIRE

by

NOREEN O'DELL

ROBERT HALE · LONDON

© Noreen O'Dell 1979
First published in Great Britain 1979

ISBN 0 7091 7549 3

Robert Hale Limited
Clerkenwell House
Clerkenwell Green
London EC1R 0HT

PHOTOSET, PRINTED AND BOUND BY WEATHERBY WOOLNOUGH,
WELLINGBOROUGH, NORTHANTS

CONTENTS

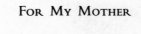

FOR MY MOTHER

ILLUSTRATIONS

Between pages 48 and 49

Between pages 96 and 97

INTRODUCTION

Hampshire, one thousand, four hundred and fifty-seven square miles of some of England's loveliest country, and probably more variety within its boundary than any other county. Hampshire Hogs they call us, but it's affectionately said, and I have never known anyone take offence at the title.

Set tidily in the centre of the south of England, with its several rivers draining into the busy seaway of the Solent, Hampshire is a maritime county, with tales to tell of naval battles and fleet reviews, of the *Mary Rose*, H.M.S. *Victory*, and the *Queen Mary*. Backed by rich and fertile farmlands, it is an agricultural county, with much of the land given over to large herds of dairy cattle and the growing of cereals.

Though steeped in history, and very conscious of its long and precious heritage, Hampshire also looks forward and is the home of some of the world's most advanced industry and technology. Add for good measure the New Forest, sandy beaches, and some of the finest trout fishing to be found anywhere, and it is clear that here is a portrait well worth the painting.

Much of its structure is chalk downland, east-west folds of varying height, outlying ripples of the great collisions from which the Alps were formed in a young Earth. These shaven green mounds, with their often dramatic white-faced escarpments, spread in a wide band across the north of the county from the western border with Wiltshire to the higher hills of 'Little Switzerland' in the east. By contrast, there are beds of clay and of sand; one such sandy strip edges the eastern boundary, at the end of the Sussex Weald, and a similar area of poor soil in the opposite corner surprisingly supports the great expanse of the New Forest. The southern shores are an unspectacular mixture of pale yellow sand and small shingle, with large natural harbours in the east surrounding the two islands of Hayling and Portsea, and sea-cliffs rising higher towards Dorset.

This wide contrast of habitat makes Hampshire a naturalists' delight, since it attracts a correspondingly large variety of flora and fauna, giving a choice of sea-water, salt-marshes, mudflats, ponds, bogs, fresh-water streams, deciduous and coniferous woodland, rolling downs and open heath.

Apart from several small tributaries in the north, which flow into the larger rivers of Berkshire and Surrey, Hampshire's rivers flow southwards, among them the clear chalk angling-waters of the Meon, Itchen and Test, and, more familiar to yachtsmen, the Hamble, Beaulieu and Lymington. The Avon was also ours at one time, and indeed still is in part, but the re-organisation of county boundaries in 1974 robbed us of the river-mouth at Christchurch. A large triangular chunk of Hampshire became Dorset overnight, taking with it a length of coastline from Highcliffe to Bournemouth and its hinterland.

Despite this loss, the population of Hampshire continues to grow, with a great surge of development in almost all areas; an increased population still has to be fed and housed, educated, employed, and occupied in its leisure hours. The towns most affected are Basingstoke and Andover in the north, but massive changes are taking place elsewhere, and the major cities of Southampton and Portsmouth, together with the smaller market towns, face enormous expansion. Motorway systems too have altered the landscape, and more is threatened if the M3 is finally completed.

A variety of soils and a long growing season, combine to provide a wide choice of home-grown produce. The coastal area is well-known for its generally temperate climate, much of the land being sheltered from the most severe conditions by the Isle of Wight. The hills around Winchester, not really very high, are often spattered with a shower of snow that has not touched Southampton, only nine miles south. Hampshire rarely sees snow between early April and mid-November, and a winter with no fall at all is not unusual. A county average of 1600 sunny hours and 32.5 inches of rain, compare favourably with the national figures of 1475 hours and 35.9 inches. The many springs hidden under the chalk proved a blessing in 1976, when the water supply during the drought conditions was much less critical than in other areas.

Cereal is our main crop, mainly wheat, with some barley, oats, maize – and a great increase lately in oil-seed rape. The south-facing slopes near Petersfield support a thriving vineyard, which produces a most pleasant pale dry wine. In the areas of mixed soils away from the chalk, vegetables and fruit come into their own, with tomatoes and flowers grown under glass. Some twenty per cent of this horticultural land is used for nursery stocks, with some of the largest stock-producers in Europe based in Hampshire. Even the county's chalk rivers are productive, and account for half the watercress market for the whole country.

Livestock is varied; in 1977, Hampshire grassland supported eight hundred dairy herds of up to seventy cows; and sheep, once the basis of downland farming but reduced in numbers during recent years, are again on the increase. Beef cattle, pigs and poultry have their place too, mainly managed by specialist farmers; and the rivers and sea yield their own protein-rich produce, salmon and trout, eels, bass, mullet and mackerel, oysters, crab and lobster.

Pupils and students come from all over the world for places at the public schools of Winchester and Bedales, and for higher education at technical colleges and at the University of Southampton, which has grown to enormous proportions from very modest beginnings, and now caters for nearly 6000 students.

The normal scope of employment in Hampshire is widened by the numerous factory premises contained on industrial estates around many towns, and by such world-wide concerns as I.B.M., Esso and British-American Tobacco, plus the commercial docks at Southampton, and branches of the Armed Forces, all of which are well represented in the county.

Literary and historical figures of the past are prominent in Hampshire's story. Gilbert White studied the natural history of his beloved village at Selborne, and wrote his famous book which has run to many editions since its first publication in 1788; William Cobbett rose from ploughboy to politician, living much of his life at Botley where he wrote his *Rural Rides*; others include Jane Austen, Charles Kingsley and Charles Dickens, and Isaac Watts, whose hymns are a part of our lives. The Duke of Wellington, Lord Nelson, Lord Palmerston, General Gordon, Lord Baden-Powell, and

Florence Nightingale, are all Hampshire people, by birth or at least by association.

What about Hampshire's own history? There is much, as proven by the many barrows, tumuli and earthworks, together with a wealth of implements in flint and bronze, displayed in our museums. The Romans made a deep impression here during nearly half a millennium of occupation, leaving behind them roads, walls and forts so well built that they remain, in part, today. The hotch-potch of continental invaders who followed them destroyed much that was in their barbarous path, but with the rise in importance and prosperity of Winchester, the chosen seat of kings, and the development of the port at Southampton, Hampshire's story becomes clearly traceable, right through to the twentieth century.

It is not possible to include all the points of interest in such a county as Hampshire; people must see for themselves the quaint corners, unexpected views and pockets of history and beauty, just waiting to be discovered.

I

WINCHESTER

One morning in early December, I set out to climb St Catherine's Hill at Winchester, an activity more usually reserved for warmer seasons. The night had bequeathed a thick hoarfrost to the heart of Hampshire, and the narrow chalk path was slippery with ice. The hill which rises steeply from beside the busy A33, has a gradient of 1-in-3 in places, and the ascent was a perilous, scrambling affair. I arrived at the top glowing and breathless, but the effort was well rewarded. For once, not surprisingly perhaps, I had the hill to myself, and I might have been alone in the world; on that morning it was a world of great beauty, a pure land of sparkling white – each leaf, each twig and every blade of grass lace-edged, of jewelled green where the sun had reached, with a sky of clear blue and gold above.

The valley on the south side looked still half-asleep, filled with white vapoury shadows, for the sun was behind the next ridge, warming the downs that rolled away to the sea-lanes of the Solent. From the gently sloping crown, 230 ft above the road,* I watched the traffic streaming silently away northeastwards, to beechwood country, fairly flat at first but rising steeply as it nears the Surrey border to form spectacular tree-clad hangers.

The west face of the hill, sloping so steeply away, gave a wide, panoramic view. To the left, huge white scars in the chalk showed the extent of a new building site at Olivers Battery, where once the hills echoed to the crash of Cromwell's cannon. The downland disappeared into a frosty mist, but I could imagine, in the miles behind it, the early-winter colours of the beautiful New Forest, and the rich farmlands of the Test Valley.

From the foot of St. Catherine's Hill, across the river, spread that age-old city, Winchester, one-time capital of all England.

* 328 ft (99.97m) above sea-level.

Landmarks in the patchwork of old and new were easily identified – the cathedral, long and low, the grey buttresses of the College Chapel, and beside the water-meadows, the unique quadrangle of St Cross, whose sombre-toned bell chimed the hour across the crisp air; on the sky-line beyond the rooftops were the more recent buildings of the expanding town, the red brick mass of the county hospital, the prison tower, and newer still, the great glass rectangle of the police headquarters.

Winchester has settled comfortably over the centuries into this hollow surrounded by gentle mounds of Hampshire's famous downland, the foundation of the south's prosperity; for St Catherine's forms the western spur of the South Downs, and it was the quality of the sheep grazing this springy chalk turf that gave the medieval world some of its finest and most sought-after woollen cloth. The valley between St Catherine's Hill and Hockley was put to macabre use during the great plague of the mid-1300s, when vast numbers of Winchester's citizens – half its population – were buried there in a mass grave.

The hill of St Catherine, thought to have been named after the martyr, Catherine of Alexandria, was probably the original settlement from which the greater community grew, and may indeed be one of the earliest sites of permanent habitation in the country. It was to the south coast that the first explorers sailed from the continent, and inlets leading to a safe anchorage and suitable landing site must have been eagerly sought. Hampshire has its share of such rivers, and the Itchen is one of them, flowing between the hill and the city on its way to Southampton Water. Along this waterway ventured the men of the Iron Age, some 600 years BC. The hill would have appealed to them both for its strategic and economic advantages, and there they settled. The community seems to have been more or less self-supporting, for relics found during the 1920s suggest that they cultivated the land, and grew cereal which they ground into rough flour using stone querns; they kept cattle, pigs and sheep, made pottery by hand, and spun yarn with primitive spindle whorls.

During the first century BC, the hillfort was abandoned suddenly, perhaps over-run by a new invader, for Belgic adventurers swarmed through the area at that time, but the ramparts of that Iron Age earthwork can still be traced. Over the years, various changes have been seen on the crown of the hill. A medieval chapel was built, and has long since disappeared, but a strange miz-maze of uncertain origin still exists, cut deeply into the turf. For several hundreds of years a clump of beech trees has decorated the summit, the present group having been planted by a local camp of militia in 1762, and 'renewed' in 1897

Now the area belongs to Winchester College, and is a scheduled Site of Special Scientific Interest, administered by the county's Naturalists' Trust. Rabbits roam the fifty-seven acres, habitat of stonechats, tits and finches; in the summer a great variety of butterflies feast among the many flowers, said to include some rare orchids, that flourish on the chalkland.

Winchester has seen a number of immigrant communities, for after the Belgii came the Romans, who established their neat, geometric town west of the Itchen; the streets of today's city are still set out on those original lines of nearly 2,000 years ago. The Romans arrived soon after the conquest of the year 44, and called their town Venta Belgarum, town of the Belgii. With true Roman efficiency, they organised a temporary earth rampart behind which to build their homes in safety, and set up their town; then they began to rebuild the fortifications in stone. They made a gateway at five main points, plus perhaps one smaller opening. The town developed quickly into an administrative centre serving a wide area, and by the end of the first century Winchester was the fifth largest walled city in Roman Britain.

From each of the gates, they built a road, radiating across the countryside to the other Roman settlements in the south, and these well-laid trackways are to some extent, still in use. The road south leads to Southampton and the river-mouth; others were directed westwards towards Salisbury and to Wales; eastward to Portchester; and northward, probably Hampshire's busiest road today, to Basingstoke and then to London, though in Roman times its destination was Silchester, of little importance now.

If the roads have survived, sadly none of the buildings have done so, but there is a wealth of evidence of Roman ways of life in the City Museum, together with some almost-complete floor mosaics. Without doubt there is a great deal more waiting to be found, but the ground level has risen several feet over the centuries, and excavation could only be made by demolishing the city centre!

The sudden departure of the legionaires back to Rome left Winchester without government and it soon decayed; by the fifth century it was a ghost town.

Winchester's next years are enveloped in a historical twilight, until in 849 in the Berkshire town of Wantage an infant was born who was to become the leading figure in Wessex, and farther afield.

Alfred, son of a king and pupil of the learned Swithun, became king himself in 871, during the period of ruthless invasions by the Vikings. Alfred was a courageous warrior and a wise ruler, a combination which brought peace to Wessex, for so long torn by strife. He caused the tumbledown Roman walls to be repaired and rebuilt, and devoted his energies to the church, to learning and the arts, making Winchester an ecclesiastical and a cultural centre. He set up a Mint which lasted for 400 years, and kept the Treasury in the town. A more ordered way of life encouraged trade, and the city grew rapidly and prosperously. Soldier, churchman, statesman and educationalist, Alfred truly deserved his title of The Great.

A thousand years after his death, the citizens, led by another Alfred, the city's mayor, Alfred Bowker, acknowledged their debt to this father-figure. In 1901, Alfred Bowker caused a statue to be commissioned which stands in the Broadway, the focal-point of all Winchester. It is a splendid memorial, sculpted by Hamo Thornycroft, a larger-than-life figure in bronze, set on a great granite block, and it is said that to ensure an exact level, the whole was rested on tons of demerara sugar. It is a worthy tribute which catches exactly the rugged spirit of the Anglo-Saxon age, as Alfred the Great stands facing the city he cared for so deeply, holding his sword aloft, hilt skyward, his shield resting at his knee.

Alfred watches over the hub of the city, looking up the long narrow main street to the medieval Westgate, part of the old walls. Like most towns built for another era, Winchester has suffered badly from the motor age. After various traffic schemes had been discussed, it was decided to exclude through-vehicles, and to pave the centre section of the main road, an improvement for pedestrian browsers, and a disjointed headache for drivers.

My favourite walk starts in this paved area by the Butter Cross, the one-time market-place. It is an elegant Gothic monument, a trifle fussy perhaps, in a wedding-cake fashion, but graceful; four octagonal steps lead to the plinth on which the sculpture stands, tall, slender, and much carved. A local landowner wanted at one time to have the Cross moved to his private estate at Cranbury Park, but after his henchmen were driven off by furious citizens, he had to make do with a plaster image. The office building behind it has an unusual decor; modern indoor wall-surfaces stand side by side with old beams and stone walls of William the Conqueror's time, an intriguing mixture.

The High Street has been called 'the most interesting in the country'; whether that be true or false, it certainly encompasses just about every architectural age. Here indeed, is a place to stand and stare, at Saxon Alfred in one direction, Westgate in the other; the Butter Cross, the great wrought-iron clock hanging over the street, and opposite, the picturesque Godbegot House, a perfect example of Tudor building.

The house stands on a site which was part of the old Manor of Goudbeyete, an estate given by poor 'unready' Ethelred to his wife Emma, ten years after their marriage in 1002. The old building houses a jewellers' shop now, and upstairs, the owners have arranged a tasteful museum of suitable furniture and *objets d'art*.

Here, too, is the Georgian frontage of the *Hampshire Chronicle*, always attractive with its first floor row of window-boxes providing a splash of colour. The newspaper, established in 1772 by John Linden, was the first to be printed and published in Hampshire, and has been issued every week since, with the exception of just one edition during the General Strike of 1926. Progress of the American Civil War was reported in the *Hampshire Chronicle*, and the departure to Botany Bay of Australia's first 'settlers'; the death of Nelson at Trafalgar, and the defeat of Napoleon at Waterloo. But the accent was on local news, and a playbill invited townsfolk to visit Winchester's Theatre, inactive now, but with hopes of revival.

Through the arcade behind the Butter Cross, on the left, so tucked away that it can more easily be passed by than dis-

covered, is the tiny 'mother church' of St. Lawrence, thought
to stand on the site of the chapel of William's castle. Records
show that during the reign of Elizabeth I, it was St Lawrence's
bell that rang the city curfew, while the usual bell was being
repaired. Since 1662, it has been the custom for a new bishop to
be received at St Lawrence's before his enthronement service in
the cathedral that dominates the city. In that quiet sanctuary
he offers his private prayers, before leaving for procession to the
colourful ceremony. This practice was first recorded in 1206,
but at a different church. The last time' St Lawrence's was used
for such an occasion was in February 1975, at the enthronement of John Vernon Taylor.

The Rectory of the church was just round the corner, an old
and timbered building, but after righteousness came the thirst-
ing, and the premises are now licensed as the Eclipse Inn.

I can seldom pass the door of the City Museum just across
the road, without going inside, for all the history of
Winchester and the surrounding countryside is held within its
three storeys, from the rough-hewn flints of Paleolithic man,
who wandered across the downs long before the habitation of
St. Catherine's Hill, to a turn-of-the-century Tangye steam
engine, and much from the ages between.

The south windows of the museum overlook the cathedral,
and there are only a few tree-lined yards to the west door. It is
not, in my opinion, a beautiful cathedral from the outside.
Dignified maybe, and rather grand, but not beautiful. Its tower
reaches only to 140 feet, and it is said, at 556 feet, to be the
longest Gothic cathedral in the world. However, the interior
makes compensation for any lack of enthusiasm about the
outside. Indeed, it is its very length that makes the nave so
breathtaking, and looking upward to the graceful arches,
supported by lofty, clustered pillars, you wonder how it could
ever have been thought 'low'. Turning to look at the west wall,
you realise that you would be wrong to dismiss it as unimpres-
sive, for with the light behind it, the great six-hundred-
year-old coloured window shows to glorious advantage.

The Friends of the Cathedral claim that there may have
been a church here since 164, built by Christian Romans, but
the building known as the Old Minster dated from about 648.
One of the earliest bishops to serve the church was Swithun, a
saintly and much-loved man. At his death in 862, he expressed

the wish that he should lie in a grave under the open sky, so that his countrymen should walk freely over it, and the rain fall upon it. And this was done, but a hundred years or so later, when Swithun was canonised, it was considered more fitting that his bones should rest inside the minister, in a grand shrine. Legend has it that Swithun's sadness takes the form of forty days of rain, starting from 'his' day, the 15th of July.

When William conquered the south, he had a new minster built, just to the south of the existing building (which site was excavated recently with much interest), and it is William's cathedral that we see today, repaired, improved and altered. Whether you wander for your own pleasure, or buy a guide at the well-stocked book-corner, there is much to see. My own favourite features include the font, a massive square of carved black marble, brought from Tournai in the Middle Ages. Seven such basins were brought to England, and four of them are to be found in Hampshire. At this font the infant Henry III was baptised in 1207.

In the north aisle too, thousands of feet walk over the gravestone of Jane Austen, who died in Winchester in 1817 at the young age of forty-two. A tribute from her family is engraved on the flag, but they did not consider her novels important enough to mention. Her followers think otherwise, and a brass plaque on the north wall tells her full story.

I like too, the beautifully carved choirstalls, said to be the oldest in England, and the impressive Bishop's Chair beside them. The reredos of the High Altar is superb, a vast carved wall of exquisitely sculpted figures. Another favourite is the Isaak Walton window in the south transept, where in the bottom right-hand corner, this contented fisherman sits reading by the Itchen, one of his best-loved trout streams, his tackle discarded beside him, and the hill of St. Catherine in the background; the window bears the pleasing Thessalonians' text 'Study to be Quiet'.

The Itchen plays an important part in the affairs of the city, situated as it is on the flood plain; that the cathedral is not immune was discovered rather forcefully in 1905, when the architect made his routine report on the condition of the building, and pointed out one or two defects which he considered needed rectifying. Subsequent investigations found that the entire building site was flooded with water that ebbed and flowed with the seasons, and that the cathedral was sinking on its rotting timber foundations. The repairs took six years and seven months to complete, and cost £113,000, an enormous sum in those thrifty days. The work necessarily involved an army of workmen, but the hero of the day was the diver, William Walker, who worked alone under the great church, under-pinning, repairing and strengthening. Wearing his diver's outfit weighing nearly 200 lbs, he personally handled an estimated 25,800 bags of concrete, 114,900 concrete blocks, 900,000 bricks, and squeezed 500 tons of grouting into the cracked walls. William Walker has been called dramatically, but not untruthfully, 'the man who saved Winchester Cathedral', and earned himself a burial place within. The river is still a problem, and visitors may only see the crypt 'water level permitting'!

I like to leave the church by the south door leading to the Close and the fifteenth-century gateway of Cheyney Court, a most attractive corner of timbered and mellow stone buildings. This leads to College Street, where in one of the houses Jane Austen died after coming to Winchester from her home in Chawton for medical treatment.

An archway through the street's buttressed walls, lit in places with tiny fourteenth-century windows, leads to the Porter's Lodge of Winchester College, a snug room with walls nearly a yard thick, for those were turbulent days, and folk had not forgotten the upheaval and violence of the Peasants' Revolt. This ancient College was founded during the reign of Richard II, in October 1382, by William of Wykeham. A great church-man and statesman – twice Chancellor of England, Wykeham held the bishopric of Winchester from 1367 until his death in 1404, long years in which he did much for the city. His is one of the grandest tombs in the cathedral, in the south aisle, but the College itself is his real memorial, and the 'old boys' are known as 'Wykehamists'.

The teaching of boys by the clergy was a long-accepted practice, but Wykeham had approached the whole subject of learning with thought and foresight. Winchester College was to take care of the first part of a boy's education, after which he would graduate to Wykeham's other major foundation, New College, Oxford. Numerous books have been written about the College history, and records of the pupils' meals, accommodation and timetables make interesting and often salutary reading. Today's boys, in their uniforms of Oxford blue, must be thankful to live in the twentieth century.

Visitors are allowed in parts of the College and its grounds, and a path leads through to the playing-fields beside the Itchen, and beyond to a riverside walk in either direction. To the south, the path can be followed across verdant water-meadows to St Cross, a unique establishment consisting of a quadrangle of grey stone buildings. The Hospital of St. Cross was set up by Henri de Blois, brother of King Stephen, and grandson of the Conqueror, for the succour of 'thirteen poor ... men ... so reduced in strength ... rarely able to raise themselves without the assistance of another'. The almshouses form one of the four sides, a terrace of neat stone dwellings with red-tiled roofs and fourteen tall round chimneys. The resident 'brethren' wear robes of black with a silver cross, or of claret with a 'Beaufort badge', depending on their order, and flat, medieval-style hats, which apparel looks not at all out of place when the men go about their business in today's city.

The Norman church forms one corner of the quadrangle, sturdy, plain, and cruciform in shape, with a squat tower. A great dip in the 'doorstep' bears witness to the generations of feet which have entered the church, attended daily by the brethren for the matins, and visited constantly by tourists. The lofty roof is supported by massive round pillars, each fourteen feet round and fourteen feet high. Tiers of round-arched windows in the east wall contain delicately coloured fifteenth-century glass, and tiles on the floor round the font have lain there since a century earlier.

The third side forms a Tudor-style ambulatory, joining the gateway tower of Cardinal Beaufort, who succeeded Wyke-ham to the bishopric in 1404. Visitors can be escorted to the Cardinal's dining-hall, and to the kitchens where medieval cooks and scullions toiled at the huge ovens, using a great roasting-spit and an old sink served by water hauled up from the Itchen-streams directly beneath. At the gateway, footsore travellers throughout nearly 800 years have called for refresh-ment of bread and ale which was never refused them, a custom still observed in token form.

Such a walk from the College requires an afternoon's free-dom, and those with less time to spare will instead have to turn left, back along the path edging the river, to the town, past the picturesque old mills to the hump-bridge behind Alfred's statue.

At the other end of the city, the Westgate stands guard, one of the entrances through the fortifications built in the twelfth century, probably on the site of the original Roman gateway to the west. A fortress with a varied history, the Westgate is now a small museum, and a fine view is to be had from the roof, especially of the Great Hall only a stone's throw away, all that remains of the medieval castle, most of which was destroyed by Cromwell's men.

There is a marked atmosphere here, in the Great Hall, a historical presence beneath the high arched timbers, and within the flint walls lit by coloured windows. Eight pillars of fluted Purbeck marble support the roof now, and a more-than-life-size Queen Victoria, sculpted in bronze, looks down from her high platform. The fine statue was presented to Hampshire in 1887 to mark the Queen's Jubilee, but there is a feeling that no one knows quite what to do with it now.

One of Winchester's main tourist attractions hangs on the west wall, that magnificent piece of craftsmanship known as King Arthur's Round Table, with the legend that it was the very table round which that noble company of knights forgathered to arrange their chivalrous affairs. But legends are best left alone, for in their very mystery lies the essence of their charm. Sadly, in 1976, the Table was taken down from the wall for investigation, and science, that great spoil-sport, went to work; now all the world knows that, table-top though it certainly was, it has nothing to do with that romantic monarch of old. The final report has still to be made public, but it has been suggested that the wood probably dates from the 1330s. Whatever the outcome, it is a splendid piece of workmanship, and worthy of fame in its own right. The great oaken circle measures eighteen feet across, and weighs one and a quarter tons. Until the early 1500s it was unpainted, but Tudor Henry took pride in showing this piece of history to his visitors, and had the bareness covered, so that it is now striped green and yellow, dartboard fashion, with script round the edge, a Tudor Rose in the centre and a portrait of the ubiquitous king.

For centuries, the Hall housed the Assize Court for the county, and the Round Table hung above the judge's chair;

probably the best known of all to preside over the court lists was the cruel Judge Jeffreys, meting out his vicious sentences.

With the unprecedented increase in legal activity over the last few years, and changes in the court system, the Hall became hopelessly outdated; modern amenities were non-existent. Building work began, adjoining the east end of the Castle, and in February 1974, the new Crown Courts were opened by Lord Hailsham, then Lord High Chancellor. The planners seem to have been determined to make up for the years of frugal accommodation, for the complex is quite sumptuous, and the entrance foyer worthy of any Grand Hotel, lofty and spacious, with mosaic floor and clusters of hanging orange lights. There are eight vast courts, with ample facilities for the judges, lawyers, police and public. Each court, discreetly accessible from long, wide corridors, is all wood-panelled and carpeted throughout in russet tones. Winchester's Crown Courts must surely rate among the most splendid in the land. Only the atmosphere of the Great Hall is lacking.

Those defendants deprived of their liberty to leave through the front doors, are taken to the warren of cells below, and thence by Her Majesty's transport to the prison half a mile or so away on West Hill. There has been a county gaol at Winchester since the Middle Ages, occupying various sites, but the present brick building with its white tower was raised in the middle of the nineteenth century, and houses between five and six hundred prisoners, mostly serving short-term sentences, with a Remand Centre for young offenders.

It seems rather like rubbing salt in the wound to have the new Police Headquarters right next door, but this great block, already on a hill, stands eight storeys high, and is a landmark for miles around. It was started in 1962 and finished three years later. The gathering of the several independent Forces working within the Hampshire boundary under one county umbrella took place in 1967, with obvious advantages, and perhaps less obvious disadvantages. In principle there must be greater efficiency and improved communications; but somehow, some-where along the line, loyalties and local pride get lost when small groups are swallowed by larger ones, and the feeling of continuity, together with that vital personal touch, is gone forever.

The Health Service too, has been affected by this 'streamlining', and with it, the county's hospital, a Victorian building also on West Hill. Winchester's hospital was the first such establishment outside London, and started life in two small cottages at the other end of town in 1737. It moved later to improved premises, where a sedan chair (which can be seen in the City Museum) was used to convey patients. In due course, these premises too became inadequate, and in 1864, after the architect's plans had been approved by that arch-administrator Florence Nightingale, the present building was opened; four years later, Queen Victoria gave the Royal Assent, and the hospital was known henceforth as the Royal Hampshire County Hospital.

King Charles II had great plans for West Hill. He considered moving his 'capital' back to Winchester, and chose a site adjoining the castle ruins for a fine new palace; it was to be a very grand affair, a sort of English Versailles, and was designed by Christopher Wren. Work began in 1683, and construction was almost finished two years later; but then Charles died, and the work stopped. Wren's plans are on display in the City Museum. The expensive building was used variously for prisoners of the endless wars of the next years, and in 1796, became a barracks. For a hundred years it was so used, until it burned down; but it was rebuilt, and was opened again in 1898 by the Prince of Wales. The Greenjackets Regiment occupy the barracks now, and have a fine military museum which is open to the public.

Indeed, visitors have a choice of two such museums, for Winchester is the home of the Royal Hampshires. This regiment has its headquarters in the elegant Serles House, an attractive Georgian mansion set back from the road in Southgate Street.

Looking from west to east, a green backcloth to the city is formed by the hill of St Giles, the other of Winchester's two famous landmarks. The area had its heyday in the twelfth and thirteenth centuries, when a great trade fair was held there annually, a tremendously important international event at which South Down wool played a substantial part. The fair attracted merchants and craftsmen from all over Europe and beyond, but then the wool staple (or market), a vital factor, was moved from Winchester to Calais, an overwhelming blow to the neighbourhood. It was a bad time for the county;

Winchester was badly affected by the plague, and when, during the Hundred Years' War, continental travel became a hazardous business, the fair finally faded out of the annual calendar.

Traffic thunders ceaselessly below the two hills and, inevitably, the question of motorways has been raised, causing an interminable wrangle between the get-there-quickly brigade and conservationists. The Government planned to route the M3 across the water-meadows between the present turn-off at Otterbourne, and Popham; but Winchester's residents had something to say about that. The link between the port of Southampton, and the markets of London and the Midlands, was vital, some said. It would ruin the cathedral and the college, and desecrate the Itchen Valley said others. The cost would be prohibitive; a cost in excess of £22 million was mentioned. The enquiry dragged on for more than a hundred days, and the 'riots' received national Press coverage; it was the longest haggle hitherto experienced over a motorway, starting in June 1976 and ending in June 1977. The harassed inspector went away to write his report. And Winchester waited.

II

THE NORTH-EAST

Whatever the outcome of the motorway enquiry, many travellers will continue to take the Roman road they have been using for nearly two thousand years, a straight, arrow of a road, rising and falling across the folds of the downs. The fields are coloured according to the seasons, for this is cereal country, and the picture changes through sowings of barley and winter wheat, the pale green of oats, and brilliant yellow of oilseed rape a fairly new crop in these parts. Before the harvest is gathered in, the carpet of sun-bleached gold is splashed with the scarlet of poppies, pink scabious, and more rarely now, the deep blue of cornflowers. It is sheep country too, and large flocks graze on the hill-slopes, and in the valley of the River Itchen, for the river bends here from a north-south course to east-west, and the highway crosses over a rather reedy section just before Kings Worthy.

When the signpost points to Micheldever, some miles farther north, the mile or so detour is well worth-while to explore this surprisingly large community, with its thatch and flint, and timber frames. Railway travellers on the line from Waterloo to Weymouth will know Micheldever best for its series of long tunnels, excavated beneath some of Hampshire's highest land, the Popham Beacons. One of the famous names to be remembered in the church is of the Baring family, originally from Bremen, who settled eventually at Stratton Park, near to Micheldever. In the eighteenth century, Francis Baring became one of Europe's leading businessmen and financiers, and chairman of the thriving East India Company. His son was created Lord Ashburton, a familiar Hampshire name today.

The long road bears south-east to bypass Basingstoke, but among the maze of roundabouts skirting the town's western edge is a sign to Sherborne St John, marking a pleasant route to

The Vyne, a very stately Tudor home, though without a long one-family tradition. This pleasing house of red brick was built in the early years of the 1500s, for Henry VIII's friend and Lord Chamberlain, William Sandys, a man who did not always approve the ways of his royal master. Henry paid several visits to The Vyne, taking Anne Boleyn with him on at least one occasion.

In 1569 it was the turn of Elizabeth I to stay at the house, when her host was the third Lord Sandys. But affairs of state continued to occupy the queen's mind even on this country visit, and from The Vyne she wrote a command that her Scots rival, Mary, already in custody, should have some of her liberties curtailed.

The Civil War saw the end of the Sandys family at their home. While the Roundheads were besieging the Royalist stronghold of Basing House only a few miles away, their troops were quartered at The Vyne under their commander, Sir William Waller. War is always a costly business, and the sixth Lord Sandys, no longer able to afford the great house, retired only a few years after he inherited the property in 1644, to his second home, the smaller Mottisfont, near Romsey.

The Vyne was bought by the Chute family, Chaloner Chute being a successful barrister who was wealthy enough to improve the neglected estate. Later, Horace Walpole was to be a frequent visitor. Over the years, with no direct male heir in several generations, the family became farther and farther removed, with descendants assuming the name of Chute in order to retain continuity. When Sir Charles Chute died in 1956, he bequeathed the house to the National Trust, and his widow, having removed to a smaller home, died three years later.

The Vyne's south front retains some original Tudor brickwork, but it is the north face which is more familiar, having been much photographed with its white portico, the first to embellish an English country house, and thought to have been designed by John Webb, student of Inigo Jones, in 1654. From the house, the lawns sweep down to a lake, widened artificially from the Shir, the small brook which flows through the middle on its way to join the Lodden. Trees shade the banks, and in spring the ducks potter about the great pools of golden daffodils that brighten the young green.

Treasures in the house are many – tapestries, paintings, furniture and books, and there is too, a most beautiful private chapel. One of the oldest galleries, panelled and carved from floor to ceiling, provides a perfect setting for concerts of Tudor music which are given from time to time by a group of local players. In all, The Vyne is a friendly house, with a welcoming atmosphere, open to the public, and administered by a family living in the east wing which is divided into three flats.

Only four miles northwards, just about as far as you can go in Hampshire, are the farm-fields that cover the Roman town of Calleva Atrebatum at Silchester. Unlike most Roman towns that were developed by succeeding inhabitants into continuing communities, no future was envisaged for Silchester, and when the Romans left, it fell into permanent disuse. Which is why, no doubt, one of the most complete excavations of a Roman town was made possible, giving us a great knowledge and insight into the ways of life there so long ago. As with Winchester, the site was originally Belgic; round about the time that the Three Kings were trekking across the Middle East, fugitive Atrebates from northern France were settling in the woodland that covered Northern Hampshire, woodland that has long since disappeared except for the small tract of Pamber Forest.

After the Roman invasion of 43, Calleva became an organised town built within a flint wall which formed a rough octagonal shape enclosing 107 acres. There is something decidedly awe-inspiring about touching a wall that was built, stone by stone by Roman hands almost two thousand years ago. A good length of Silchester's wall, albeit tufted with grass and dandelions, still stands sturdy and strong, with a distinctive herring-bone structure. Inside, where now cows graze the lush pasture, were houses and shops, offices, courts, a town hall and public baths. There were temples too, and, what makes Silchester particularly interesting, a small building that bore all the signs of having been a Christian church was found, only 42 feet by 33 feet, but a church nevertheless, a rarity indeed in a Roman settlement.

The cost of preserving so large an area was considered prohibitive, and the site involved much valuable farmland. And so the excavations were regretfully filled in; the past vanished again, and rural life went on. But not before detailed plans were made, and models, and all the treasures collected. On the edge of the site, a small hut, rather ambitiously called the Calleva Museum, whets the appetite with photographs, plans and a relic or two, plus a comprehensive booklet. The land was at that time within the bounds of the Duke of Wellington's estate at Stratfield Saye, and the unique collection of antiquities was given, on permanent loan, by the Duke to the country's nearest museum, which sadly for Hampshire, is at Reading. But there, just across the border, the Silchester Collection is displayed for all to see just how a Roman community lived in Britain.

This well-wooded strip of north Hampshire between the chalk downs and the Thames valley, lies generally low and flat, with a soil of clay which becomes mixed with an increasing density of sand towards the eastern end. The Vyne is only one of several of Hampshire's great houses to be found in the area; Stratfield Saye has been a ducal home since 1817.

In the spring of 1769, the Honourable Arthur Wesley was born in Dublin, the fourth child of Lord Mornington, "an awkward boy" according to an alleged remark of his mother. A natural aptitude for horsemanship, and swift promotion in the British Army gave Arthur the assurance he had lacked earlier; some thirty years later, by then an experienced colonel, he reverted to his family's ancient and better-known name-spelling of Wellesley.

Another name had become prominent in French military circles; Napoleon Bonaparte. Born within four months of each other, the one in Ireland, the other in Corsica, the lives of these two brilliant soldiers were to be inextricably linked in the battleground of Europe and finally at Waterloo. For Arthur Wellesley became the Duke of Wellington, victor of 1815, hero of a nation almost delirious with relief to be free at last of the greatest threat to England since William.

A country house was sought for the Duke, making a new career for himself in politics now that peace had brought an end to his military travels. The soldier had had enough of camps, and must have a rural home; £600,000 was voted by the government for this purpose. Fourteen properties were examined, and discarded, before Stratfield Saye was chosen, not too far from – and not too near to – London. The Pitt family had owned the house, a low building which was of red brick in the seventeenth century. A hundred or so years later, the family's great-grandson, Lord Rivers, put his energies into enlarging his home, and stucco-ing the walls, giving them the terra-cotta finish there today.

The Duke's friends were surprised (and Queen Victoria none too pleased) that out of the several suggested to him, he should have settled on the unpretentious Stratfield Saye, but it is a pleasant house, with rooms moderately sized, though spacious, and surrounded by a vast estate with the River Lodden flowing through on its way to the Thames. It was the Duke's intention however, to build a grand new palace in the corner of the park, an intention which never came to fruition through that age-old restriction, lack of funds. Instead, he set about improving the smaller house, adding central-heating, and installing a water-closet in each of the bedrooms.

His Grace, the eighth Duke lives there now, Arthur Valerian, great-great-grandson of the First Duke. Realities of economy caused the decision, in 1974, to open part of the house and estate to the public. It was not only a necessity however; the Duke feels that it is "socially right" that a national heritage such as Stratfield Saye should be shared with those members of the public interested to see it. So he opened the ground floor of his house during the summer months, with all its priceless treasures, and including possessions and mementoes of the Great Duke and his associates; in the stables, left exactly as they were, an illustrated account of his life story has been arranged. It is an evocative exhibition, and you can almost hear the hooves clattering and slipping on the smooth stone floor.

The soldier's own chestnut stallion found rest and retirement there. Copenhagen, the strong and valiant charger that carried the Duke through his gruelling day of battle at Waterloo, is buried in the grounds, his grave marked with a fitting epitaph on a weathered headstone. He lies under a great Turkey oak, whose lower branches are so long and heavy that they dip to the ground, forming a very beautiful natural shroud.

The eighth Duke is both a family man, and an exceedingly busy one, with directorships, councils, trusteeships and clubs. He is involved also with the organisation of various functions, including the Royal Agricultural Show; he farms his 4,000-acre property in Spain, a gift from their government to the ancestor who fought so diligently for their freedom against the French, and manages his home estate; of these 8,000 acres he farms 2,600, and is deeply concerned with the future of agriculture. He feels too, that there is too much emphasis placed on industry and other employments, and not enough on the vital occupation of food production. Most of the Duke's land is off the chalk-belt, and his farm is chiefly concerned with cereal, beef, dairy and forestry. He is also intensely enthusiastic about the education of the sophisticated young whose life is spent mainly in a town environment, to the importance of the countryside, its industries and crafts, and whole way of life.

To this end he has opened the Wellington Country Park, which is not only a pleasure area for boating, riding and picnicking, but is developing a series of demonstrations of the crafts and products of the country – dairying, brewing, tanning, pottery making and so on, with the intention of providing eventually, a permanent living exhibition, "not only of by-gone methods," says the Duke earnestly, "but showing the vital role the countryside plays in a modern society". The battlefield of Waterloo was a long time ago; the eighth Duke of Wellington is contributing to his country's well-being in his own way.

It was through the influence of a Reverend Wellesley, one of the Duke's clerical ancestors, that the curacy of neighbouring Eversley was offered to the newly-ordained Charles Kingsley. To many, the name of Charles Kingsley means *The Water Babies* and *Westward Ho!*, but to the people of nineteenth-century Eversley he was their much-loved rector, a man of abounding energy and deep compassion, who for thirty-two years worked tirelessly among the villagers, preaching in the pulpit, teaching in the tiny school by day and holding adult classes at his home in the evening, comforting the sick, and loving his flock. To the government he was something of a thorn in its flesh, for those were days of appalling conditions among labourers, and Kingsley was an eloquent and zealous reformer.

His formal achievements too, were many. His novels, and his campaign for sanitary reform caught the attention of the Queen's Consort, Prince Albert, and he was invited to preach at Buckingham Palace and at the private chapel at Windsor, with the result that he was appointed a royal chaplain; he became Regius Professor of Modern History at Cambridge

University (where he had studied twenty years earlier without distinction), and was chosen to be a private tutor of history for 'Bertie', the Prince of Wales. In due course he was invited, with his wife, to the Prince's marriage to Princess Alexandra of Denmark – but his home was still at Eversley, and he hurried there after the Windsor ceremony to join in the villagers' festivities.

In 1873, a letter from Mr Gladstone offered this remarkable man the canonry of Westminster, which a gratified Charles Kingsley accepted. But only two busy years later, on 23rd January, he died, an event which was recorded, with regret, by Queen Victoria in her journal. Arrangements were prepared for him to be buried in Westminster Abbey, but he had earlier stated his choice to lie instead at Eversley. The Prince of Wales was represented at his funeral – and the gypsies on the Common mourned him. His grave is reached by a winding brick path in the shadow of the church to which he dedicated his full life, and is simply marked with a cross of white marble, with, in Latin, the blessed words "We love; we loved; we will love:" An epitaph worth striving for.

Inside the red-brick building, a water colour hangs on the south wall of the church as Charles Kingsley knew it, beside a brass memorial to him. His pupil and friend, John Martineau, who died only in 1910, is also remembered, and there are several plaques to members of the Cope family, long-time residents of the great house across the park.

As a young curate, the Reverend Kingsley would have been a diffident visitor to the squire, Sir John Cope, in the magnificent Jacobean mansion of Bramshill. The first sight of this vast building, with its tall chimneys is quite spectacular, seen across rolling parkland from the lane which turns off the B3011 from Hartley Wintney. With the evening sun glowing on the rosy brick, it looks like something from another age, and in the mists of a pale dawn it floats like a castle in a fairy-tale. The house is in view all along the straight mile-drive from the gatehouse, where a decorative bridge crosses the tiny River Hart.

The early history of the great mansion is obscure, but certainly there are references to a house there in the Domesday Book, and Sir John Foxley and "his manor of Bramshill" are mentioned in 1306. The country surrounding the park is largely conifer, gorse and broom, and it is 'the broom on the hill' which is thought to have given the estate its name.

Facts begin to emerge in the reign of James I, when the house was bought by Lord Zouche, an influential man at Court as well as an ardent horticulturist. During the seven years after 1605, he built his own grand house on the site, retaining some of the older buildings, so that one of the vaulted entrances is known still as 'the Foxley Gatehouse'. It is generally held that Lord Zouche intended to give the house to the king's elder son, Henry, but there is no real documentary evidence of this, and the young prince died in circumstances which gave rise to suspicion at the time, and never lived there.

The exterior is splendidly rich in decoration, with a south-west front containing three arches, and a semi-circular oriel window above. The three storeys are topped by a carved parapet, and there are loggias and terraces, wide steps and bay windows, with formal gardens and open parkland where white deer graze; it is all tremendously elegant. The family must have played troco at one time, a sort of lawn billiards using wooden balls and a spoon-shaped cue, for a large 'troco stone' forms the centre-piece of the rose garden.

The Cope family possessed the house from 1749 to 1935, and early in this century, Joan Penelope Cope, aged 12, wrote a diary of day to day happenings, an enchanting saga which was later published entirely uncorrected and unedited. Then the second Lord Brocket lived there, but in 1953, he too sold the house.

In Bramshill, the Home Office found an ideal setting for their Police College, an establishment for the higher training of selected officers from England and Wales, together with some from overseas. It seems strange to find metal filing cabinets, and telephones, and television sets among the old splendour, but splendour there still is, for the great house is largely unchanged despite its up-to-the-minute use. The entrance hall is still stone-flagged, and the stone screen rising from floor to ceiling holds ninety-two shields, now repainted, showing the coats of arms of owners of the house, from the de Ports around 1080, to Lord Brocket in 1937. The first three are of King James I, Prince Henry and Baron Zouche. Prominent in the hall is a huge carved chest, said to have been the very one in which the poor bride in "The Mistletoe Bough" met her sad death on her wedding day. Certainly it is big enough to have held a woman, but there is no record of any member of the Cope family having disappeared so tragically. Beside it is a photograph of a plaque found above an old fireplace during redecoration, commemorating the fact that "King Charles killed these Staggs with Sir Robert Zouche in this season 1630".

The rooms are lofty and spacious, with strapwork ceilings and marble fireplaces, wonderful, solid old furniture, famous, faded tapestries hanging on the walls, and wood-panelling from floor to ceiling. The Long Gallery, built north-to-south, is one of the longest and best in England, 127 feet 6 inches in length and 20 feet 6 inches across, with panelling throughout in deal, brushed with a feather to resemble grained oak; a door, similarly marked, leads to the Fleur de Lys room, reputed to be the most haunted room in the house, with a particular 'presence' in one corner. The splendid Long Gallery houses the library of the college, with books and pamphlets totalling 50,000, including a complete set of Acts of Parliament from 1225.

There is a collection too, of staffs and old truncheons, several hundreds, some beautifully carved and coloured, and there are cases of the cutlasses, swords and rattles used by keepers of the peace in a by-gone age. Great copper pans still line the shelves of the obsolete kitchens, but the cellars, vaulted and underground, are in use again, not for a secret tipple, but for quiet study of the microfilm library stored there.

Bramshill has its own simple chapel where regular services are held; the rector of Eversley still visits to lead the worship, retaining a spirit of continuity between the centuries. Charles Kingsley would find the squire's house not greatly changed.

This corner of north-east Hampshire lies on a flat, sandy plain, with long stretches of coniferous woodland mixed with sharp-spiked gorse, blooming yellow in patches throughout the year, heather, fern, and the rhododendrons that have spread so rapidly forming huge banks of bright mauve in the early summer.

Later in the year, for a few days in September that always seem, in my experience to be wet, cold or windy (though I am sure that statistics would prove otherwise), the peace is shattered by ear-splitting roars and whines, as supersonic aircraft streak through the autumn skies, hurtling in and out of the clouds, breaking sound barriers and world records, skimming over spectators' heads and accomplishing spine-tingling dives and rolls. For miles around, lamp-posts sprout blue or yellow signs, and all roads seem to lead to Farnborough, for the biennial Air Show.

This great exhibition of British aeronautical technology is staged before a world audience at the Royal Aircraft Establishment, a factory of research and development, science and invention unique in Europe, and probably in the world. Close on a quarter of a million visitors attended the display in 1978, to watch Tornados and Jaguars, Hawks, Harriers and many more being put through their paces, the end product of years of experience and effort.

Tragedy marred the show in 1952, when a de Havilland 110 disintegrated after a stunning eight-mile dive at high speed, killing the test pilot, John Derry and his observer, Tony Richards; thirty-one visitors also died as the wreckage plummeted into the crowd, and nearly eighty were injured.

The experimental station has been in operation since 1878, originally at Woolwich, when the War Office carried out trials with observation balloons. The establishment moved to Farnborough twenty-seven years later, and became the factory floor for all the famous pioneering names of British flying history. Balloons, kites, airships and dirigibles made their debut there, and aviation history was made on the 16th October 1908, when Colonel Cody flew his biplane for 463 yards, the first officially recognised powered flight in Britain. The names of Green, Hearle and de Havilland began to be heard.

The early years of the First World War saw a great expansion at Farnborough, and no one needs to be reminded of the R.A.F.'s heroic role in the grim years of the 1940s. Jump-jets and swing-wings have replaced the canvas and string, there are rockets instead of airships, radar in place of kites, and where the Colonel had his biplane, we have Concorde. It is a place of high-speed wind-tunnels, pilotless aircraft and missile guidance, gas-turbine propulsion, structural tests and pressure-suits – in a word, research. The best of Britain's aeronautical brains are there. I don't know if the world is a better place for Farnborough, but certainly British freedom owes the workers there, past and present, an immeasurable debt.

The rout of Sedan in 1870, during the war between France and Prussia, would seem to have little to do with present-day Farnborough, but it led to the building of an ornate church there, and the tombs beneath, of three of the Bonaparte family.

During that disastrous battle, Charles Louis Napoleon, nephew of the soldier from Corsica and self-appointed 'Emperor Napoleon III', was taken prisoner; his son, at fourteen already an enthusiastic fighter, had been removed from the battle-front, and escaped to England. The Spanish-born Empress, Eugenie, living in a Paris fraught with the turmoil of war, also fled to England, where in due course, the family were united in Kent. But only three years later Napoleon III died. Charles Louis was less a military man than a politician, but his son, Prince Louis, had the ambitions of his great-uncle, and prepared to take a commission in the British Army. In 1879 he persuaded his mother to allow him to fight in the Zulu War – and he was killed there in an ambush, aged 23.

The two tragedies, loss of husband and only son – and heir – broke Eugenie's heart. She set about building a memorial to her two loved ones, and with Queen Victoria's assistance bought an estate at Farnborough Hill, where she lived, although deeming it 'little more than a cottage' compared with her Parisian palace at the Tuileries, for forty years until her death in 1920, aged 94.

Her church was built on the hill in 1884, in the "Flamboyant Gothic' style, and she was buried there after a funeral at which King George V and Queen Mary were present, together with other European royalty. In the crypt below, reminiscent of Les Invalides, are the three tombs of highly polished, pink-mottled Aberdeen granite, each with just a name and a simple word etched in gold. On the north side, the body of Napoleon III lies in the uniform of General, with his Garter banner hanging above; opposite is his son, the brave lad who might have been Napoleon IV, overlooked by a crucifix given by his godfather, Pope Pius IX. And between them, high behind the elaborate stone altar, lies the sad Eugenie.

In 1895, at the request of the deposed Empress, the Abbott of Solesmes sent a community of French Benedictine monks to St. Michael's Abbey, to occupy the monastery next to the church. In 1947 they returned to France, and were replaced by a handful of black-robed monks from Gloucester who are there today, farming the estate's twenty-six acres, and maintaining the church buildings. Public services are held regularly in the church, and Mass is said daily in the crypt, where, in these days of expensive heating bills, the public services are also held in winter. The vault is shown to visitors at limited times, and a page of the Visitors' Book for 1973 includes the signature of the present prince, Jerome, great-grandson of Napoleon I, on a family pilgrimage from his Paris home.

As the suburbs spill over old boundaries, the adjoining communities of Farnborough and Aldershot are linked into one sprawling town. Until 1854, there was no permanent centre in England for the training of troops on a large scale, although the need for such an establishment was widely acknowledged. The ministerial decision was made at last, to utilise the flat tract of sandy heathland along the eastern edge of Hampshire for this purpose, and the tiny village of Aldershot was transformed without further delay into a vast army camp. It was barely in time; war was declared with Russia the same year, and the troops who first marched into the new barracks in May and June, marched out again soon after, bound for the miseries of the Crimea.

Although archaeology has shown that the Aldershot district had a pre-history community, and is mentioned in records of 885, there is little written evidence, and the isolated hamlet seems to have served mainly as a 'frontier post' for coaches and wagons using that desolate stretch of the London to Winchester turnpike road. The small groups of pine trees dotted among the gorse and bracken made excellent ambush-places for lurking highwaymen, and no doubt Dick Turpin made full use of them during the 1730s when plying his illegal trade along the lonely track, for he is said to have had his cottage-headquarters near Farnborough.

Today, the two communities of Aldershot and Aldershot Military Town are distinctly signposted. The civilian town has a reputation for being drab and uninteresting, but landscapers have done their work well, and the improved buildings are edged with trees, green open spaces and parks with a profusion of colourful rhododendrons.

Yet still, to most people, Aldershot means 'the army' with its barracks and married quarters, its horse-shows, tattoos and pageants, inspired and watched over by the great statue of the Duke of Wellington on horseback. Military museums abound, a dozen or more, each with a different character from Nursing to Paratroopers, and each well worth visiting. The stories of the various regiments are told with immense pride, and rightly so. Battles are refought in model form, heroic deeds recounted, mementoes exhibited, colours, uniforms, silverware and regalia displayed, for as Beaumarchais' Figaro would have us believe, 'a glorious thing is war'. Perhaps. Reading the Rolls of Honour and memorials to the fallen that line the walls in the garrison churches of Aldershot, I have my doubts.

Some five miles south, across the conifer-lined A287, lies the neat village of Crondall, best known perhaps, for its heavily buttressed Norman church. The pathway to the church door from one of its two gates is unusual, being of brick and flint, and lined on both sides with twelve pairs of lime trees. They are set close together, and are very beautiful in late spring when the sun shines through the fresh young green leaves. Yet they are almost more exquisite in winter, when a fresh fall of snow gives them a quality of pure magic.

The church is old and lofty, and has many treasures, including records dating back to 1543. The sturdy building was used as an outpost by Roundhead soldiers during the Civil War, a sacrilege that has given Crondall its most unique feature. For sometimes – just sometimes, a Cromwellian trooper is to be seen, riding his horse along the lime avenue, and disappearing into the church. Twice in this century, so they say.

The same A287 leads on to Odiham, with a long Georgian street flanked by shops and inns, and with many picturesque corners. Odiham, with helicopters puttering overhead from the nearby R.A.F. station, is a small town of mixed architectural styles, half-timbered fronts, bow-windows and pointed gables, with a great church tower rising behind the main street.

The church, built in brick on impressive lines, stands beside the Bury, the town square, and gathered round it are the old almshouses of the seventeenth century; a small cottage with a huge chimney bears the unattractive name of the Pest House, and remembers the fearful days when it housed plague victims abandoned by everyone else.

A small section of the Basingstoke Canal passes the outskirts of Odiham, and beside the tow-path, in a young coppice, stands a most unexpected ruin. It is the thirteenth-century

Odiham Castle, a new stronghold when King John set out from it bound for Runnymede, and the historic signing of the Magna Carta in the green fields there. Only a little is left now, just the ruined keep, its walls many feet thick, and lumps of flint large and small lie all around amongst the thin grass and the bracken. It was the only octagonal keep in the country. The castle was left to decay 400 years ago, and has been unoccupied since then.

Along these quiet lanes, bordered by fields of sweetcorn, sheep pastures, and hedgerows where whitethroats sing and yellowhammers flash their bright plumage, lies the village of Greywell, grey only in name, as it is built of red brick, like so many of the buildings in this part of Hampshire.

Beneath the road at the east end of the village flows the Whitewater, a clear stream padded with crowfoot, a feeding place for pied wagtails and families of mallard. June is the month for Greywell, when its mellow, higgledy-piggledy cottages are garlanded with honeysuckle, clematis, and great clusters of wistaria, with poppies on the verges, and the giant chestnut trees in front of the Dower House a mass of white 'candle' flowers. The long gravel path to the church is scented with a hedge of may, white and deep pink. It's a small church, with a pointed short spire housing four bells. The craftsman of the tenor bell which chivvies up latecomers to the service, immortalised himself by inscribing the words 'Henry Knight made me in 1662'. I think the judges of the Best Kept Village must have come to Greywell in June; they awarded the coveted prize to this little community both in 1971 and 1972.

From Greywell, it is only a short drive to one of Hampshire's most famous landmarks, the total ruins of Basing House. Until the Civil War, Basing House stood as one of the greatest showpieces in England, home of the shrewd Sir William Paulet who had seen much turmoil through four Tudor reigns, and who had survived when so many others did not, by being more 'a willow, not an oak', according to his oft-quoted remark.

The County Council has done much in recent years to preserve and restore the old ruins which are now open to the public, and which include an Iron Age earthwork and foundations of a Norman castle. Some of the decayed pink brick of the old house can be traced from the road, the ivy-covered archway with an engraved coat of arms, through which in

1554, Queen Mary drove with her new husband, the Spanish Philip, after their marriage in Winchester Cathedral; the round dovecote in the corner of the grounds, reputed to contain seven hundred nesting holes; and also the timbered front porch of the Lodge.

The grand mansion, rated second only to Windsor Castle by some, stood beside the main road from London to the west, a position of strategic and economic importance when the Civil War erupted in 1642. John Paulet, the fifth Marquess of Winchester, fortified the house against the Roundheads. A long and harrowing siege followed, with many skirmishes, which lasted for three long years; many hundreds within the house died, either from injuries received during the fighting, or from disease and starvation. The women of the house stripped lead from the roof and cast it into bullets for their menfolk to fire; a maid was killed at the side of her mistress while both were so employed. So acute was the shortage of food that the birds in the dovecote became a choice delicacy, "baked in pastry with their legs upward" according to old records.

But it was all to no avail; injury, sickness, treachery and desertion weakened the position of the gallant band that remained, and in October 1645, Cromwell's men, said to be 7,000 strong, stormed the great stronghold and breached the walls. The old Marquess was found hiding in an oven and taken to the Tower, although he was later released and exiled; nearly a quarter of a million pounds' worth of treasures were plundered from the castle before it was burned to the ground. Devastation was absolute.

The story of Basing House is one of the most courageous in our history; but what a waste of men, of ideals, of fine buildings and irreplacable treasures the whole affair of the Civil War seems to have been. But the same, I suppose, can be said of all wars.

The bustle of modern Basingstoke is just two miles away, and despite the fact that it has one of the fastest growth rates in the country, it somehow retains the indefinable air of a country town. Certainly there have been changes, with precincts and steps and walkways, but still the atmosphere persists. Only ten years ago, the little town with a long pre-Domesday history was the modest agricultural centre of a wholly rural area, but then came the Town Development Agreement between the

Greater London Council and the Hampshire County Council, and Basingstoke's future was altered at a stroke. In 1961, the population was 25,000; the number doubled in the next decade, and for 1986 the estimate is 113,000.

Industry and commerce have increased multifold, with the resulting growth also of housing, schools and entertainment facilities for the influx of new residents. Let no one in Basingstoke complain of having nothing to do. There are in excess of one hundred social organisations available to enthusiasts, from Philately, Silver Bands and Rifle Shooting, to Chess, Bellringing and Chrysanthemums; and Basingstoke also has that great advantage, a theatre, The Haymarket in old Wote Street, which stages the revues, musicals and repertory plays so sadly missed elsewhere these days.

A cloth industry was once the town's claim to mild prosperity, and the canal which was opened in 1789 between the Wey and the Thames carried the merchandise to London with barges conveying timber and coal. The opening of the railway line in 1839 caused the end of canal traffic, and the waterway fell into disuse. The 1970s have found a different interest in the canal network, and an energetic force of volunteers has been working in its spare time to clear and re-open the long stretch of water for leisure use.

Basingstoke is a major station on the main line from Waterloo to the west, and rail travellers can see, on a hill, the ruins of the Holy Ghost Chapel in a small cemetery, thought to have been established in the reign of King John. It is one of Cromwell's ruins, torn down for ammunition in the Civil War.

The parish church of St. Michael has the unusual situation of being settled in a dip, instead of the more unfamiliar choice of a rise of land; built in the early sixteenth century by Bishop Fox in yellow-grey stone, it has a fine pinnacled tower, but the interior is rather barren apart from some elaborate woodwork. Cromwell's forces were active here too, and used the church to stable their horses and store gunpowder, ready for the attack on Basing House; but the magazine blew up and severely damaged the building. The east end suffered in the Second World War as well, and the lovely stained-glass windows were lost.

Some of Basingstoke's oldest buildings are the almshouses in London Street, and the brick and timber-framed Elizabethan cottage opposite the church. A good example of ancient and modern, the church has the sixteenth-century cottage on one side, and a high brick wall edging a new shopping precinct on the other.

Most of the town's history is contained in the Willis Museum at the end of New Street; the museum was founded in 1931 by a local clock and watch-maker who was born in 1877, and died in 1970. Mr Willis loved clocks, and made horology his work and his hobby; his collection formed the basis of the museum and it still has a large corner devoted to timepieces dating from 1575.

There is a seventeenth-century replica made from a drawing by Galileo of his father's invention; and the workings of the Town Hall clock of 1700 are there too. But the museum is not only of clocks, fascinating though they are; there are sections for natural history, geology, archaeology, pottery, coins, and temporary exhibitions of various forms of art.

The road south borders the estate of Hackwood Park, home of Lord Cadman, and leads to Lasham, whose airfield has become Britain's biggest training centre for glider pilots since its small beginnings in the 1950s, and has developed into what may be the largest unsubsidised gliding mecca in the world. Lasham is known to enthusiasts in all continents, and is a frequent venue for championships. With nearly one hundred gliders of light wood and fibreglass, any suitably fine day in summer sees club members on flights of up to three hundred miles, swooping and rising on the air-currents that support them on their silent travels; they return as heat from the westering sun loses strength, and upcurrents settle into stillness. Sometimes a pilot will miscalculate, and that's when a team of his friends sets off with a road trailer to the distant field in which the graceful bird made its bumpy landing.

At Bentley, between Farnham in Surrey and Alton, that happy pair Robert and Olave Baden-Powell found their 'perfect home', and they settled there for many years between the two world wars. From the house they called Pax Hill, they furthered their great joint interest of Scouting and Guiding with immense energy, and became much involved in parish affairs; the village sign on the main road was Lord Baden-Powell's idea, and takes the form of an 'open book', showing a map of the district painted on one 'page' and points of local interest on the other – with a Boy Scout depicted in the corner.

Being many years her husband's junior, the young Olave was destined for a long widowhood, during which she carried on their life's work with never-failing cheer, always ready with her wide, infectious smile. She did not return after his death to live at Bentley, but visited it often from her home at Hampton Court, retaining a lively interest in the village until her death in 1977.

A mile or so south, Viscount Montgomery, veteran of many wartime campaigns, lived in retirement at the picturesque Isington Mill, on the banks of the River Wey.

When travelling by train through Hampshire as a child, I can remember the feeling of apprehension that stole over me when I saw the large painted signs along the embankments "Take Courage", and "You are entering the Strong Country". I used to wonder what perils I was about to face, but as no disaster ever befell me, the whole thing was rather inexplicable. I did not know for many years that they were advertisement hoardings for beer. Mine was not a drinking family.

This central-eastern area was brewing country, with the large hop-gardens on fertile upper greensand providing a livelihood for some, and seasonal perks for many others, when casual labour, often the same faces year after year, arrived to gather the mature crop from tall support poles and fill the wicker baskets – and then wonder how to get rid of the green-brown stains on their hands.

The town at the heart of all this activity was Alton, straddling a long, winding street, part of the old road from the capital to the west. Sadly, oast-houses and commercial hop-growing belong to Hampshire's past; there are a few left, and stray plants can be seen climbing in a roadside hedgerow. The only beer brewed in the town now is Harp Lager, but lager requires a different process from traditional beer, and the seedless hops that are used are mainly imported from Germany.

Memories of the old days are brought to life in the Curtis Museum in the main street, founded in 1855 by Dr William Curtis, a medical man and keen botanist; it provides a splendid narrative of the industry, domesticity and entertainment of a by-gone Alton. The town has had some notable residents; an ivy-covered frontage also in the main street shows where John Henry Newman lived for three years, before he became a

Cardinal and leading spokesman of Victorian days; and Edmund Spenser is said to have written some of his sixteenth-century poetry in a house in Amery Street.

Alton was in the thick of the Civil War, and even the church tells its own story of fighting and bloodshed. Many wooden church doors are pitted with age, but few are pitted with bullet holes, as Alton's are; in the stone walls beside the door, bullets are said to be still embedded. For St Lawrence's was the final sanctuary of eighty Royalists, trapped by General Waller's Parliamentarians; many died there, some surrendered, and Colonel Richard Boles, sword in hand, was driven back and back till there was nowhere left but the pulpit; and there he was slain.

St Lawrence's is an old grey church, with a spire, built soon after William's conquest, and the tower and one or two other parts are original. An unusual feature is the double nave and chancel, the smaller southern nave with a rounded Norman arch being encompassed by the newer fabric. Everywhere in the town there are memories of the Civil War; the small street leading to the church contains a row of low brick almshouses, with red-tiled roofs and leaded windows, and the plaque "Founded by Thomas Geale J.P. A captain in Cromwell's army".

The important complex of Treloar's Hospital spreads on the western outskirts of Alton. London-born William Treloar, lively son of a Helston clerk, possessed the rare combination of ideals of thought, and the ability for practical application. At the age of fifty, Treloar's success in public life grew alongside his interest in London's poor and disabled children; in due course he was knighted, and in 1906, he became Lord Mayor of London. This exalted position enabled Sir William to fulfil a dream – an establishment "curative and educational" for London's "little cripples". He asked for £60,000. His mayoral year realised £70,000, contributed by street hawkers, pugilists and actors, politicians, lords and ladies, even King Edward and Queen Alexandra. A member of the staff of the *Daily Telegraph* knew of some derelict hospital huts at Alton, left over from use in the South African war. In 1908, Treloar's Hospital was born, specialising in the treatment of tuberculosis and disability in children, combining medical care with training for their future. By the time Sir William died in 1923, aged eighty, 3,642 children had passed through 'Treloar's'.

The hospital has been rebuilt and enlarged; there are facilities for sport and outdoor activities, teaching, encouraging, broadening outlook and confidence. Nowadays orthopaedic surgery is carried out there with patients of all ages. There has been talk for years about closing down Treloar's, and incorporating it into the larger hospitals of the Health Service, and the talk goes on. So does Treloar's. The hospital has a tremendous atmosphere of cheer and wisdom, as though Sir William still watches there. Perhaps he does. Long may he do so.

Some two miles to the south, the charming village of Chawton, neat, tree-shaded and prosperous looking, lies at the junction of the Winchester and Portsmouth roads to London, both busier in earlier centuries than now. The passing horse-drawn traffic must have provided Jane Austen with a good deal of interest as she watched from the windows of the cottage at the apex of the two roads.

The situation was ideal for a posting inn, and during the reign of William III, a plain, square house was built there, with a yard behind it for the horses and vehicles. The house was on the estate of Chawton Manor, and later became a private dwelling. When Jane Austen's brother lived at the Manor, he made alterations and improvements to the 'cottage', and invited his widowed mother to live there with his two sisters, Jane and Cassandra, an invitation which they were happy to accept. Jane was thirty-four at that time, and the small family settled there, after several changes of address, in July 1809. And so they remained, but eight years later, Jane became increasingly unwell, and left to seek medical advice in Winchester; unsuccessfully, for sadly, she did not return.

Her pithy novels, amusing and of great charm, have won for her a devoted following, and a Memorial Trust ensures that her posthumous affairs are properly conducted. The brick cottage has been restored as far as possible (having in the meantime been used as dwellings for three labouring families) to its condition when she lived there, and is open to the public as a museum. Perhaps 'museum' is not the right word, for the house is still essentially Jane Austen's home. Set among the gardens she tended, where her favourite flowers grow along the edges of a wide sweep of lawn, the house captures her very character. Each room displays her possessions, and many will be familiar to those who know her work well, for Jane frequently drew material for her stories from her own life. She wrote three of her six novels while living at Chawton, mostly in secret, listening always, for the creaking of a particular door which gave her sufficient warning of a visitor's approach to enable her to hide her work.

The piano is open, with a music sheet for a boulanger ready for the dance; her niece wrote that Jane had "a natural taste" and played "very pretty tunes". An inlaid box containing ivory letters waits for nimble fingers to play word-games, for Jane played often with her young relatives. Her work-box and 'huswif' are ready for use, and she was a neat and skilful needlewoman, as a scarf and a handkerchief on display testify; in her bedroom overlooking the garden, is a patchwork quilt worked by Jane and her mother. There are pictures and prints on all the walls, some of the Duke of Wellington at the peak of his career, and many concerning naval matters, for the Austen brothers were noted seamen. But perhaps the most enchanting of all are the parts of manuscripts, the notes and letters, written in her own hand to her family and friends – snippets of gossip and the chit-chat of domestic trivia, all spiced with that delicious dry humour that so delights her readers. These, to me, make Chawton such a joy.

Another home-turned-into-museum is The Wakes, a few minutes drive away at Selborne, where Gilbert White lived his happy eighteenth-century life. A dedicated and meticulous naturalist, his classic book *The Natural History of Selborne* was published in 1788, the first of many editions.

He was curate of Selborne too, grandson of the vicar; he could never be vicar himself, being an Oxford man, for the living was, by virtue of land ownership, reserved for a graduate of Cambridge.

The Wakes has been turned into an educational centre, with the accent on wildlife and the eighteenth century. It places helpfully into perspective other personalities of the era who were famous in their own fields in Hogarth, Gainsborough, Reynolds and Turner; Handel; Bonnie Prince Charlie, Captain Cook, General Wolfe, and Clive of India. There is some fine furniture too, showing the elegance and craftsmanship of Sheraton, Hepplewhite and Chippendale. But as at Chawton, the most evocative room is the study where Gilbert White's own possessions are set out, as he would have used them. In this comfortable, peaceful room, he attended to the affairs of his parish and of his house. On the writing-table are his ink-stand and quill pen, and candlesticks, indicating that he often worked late into the night. There are account books marked 'personal' and 'household', recording such bills as "window tax to L. Day 1760 1.2.6., waistcoat lining 5.9, and blacksmith's bill 8.9", plus the rather frivolous and endearing item "spent at Selborne fair 6d." There are sermons too, prepared for the pulpit in his ancient church just across the village green.

From the windows of his study, Gilbert White looked out across the tranquil lawns to magnificent beech-clad hangers which were among his favourite haunts, and where he did much of his natural studying. He died in 1793, and is buried in a simple grave overlooking the dipping slopes he loved so well, marked with a modest "G.W. 1793". Behind the enormous and incredibly old yew, with its tired branches resting on the ground, is the church's west window, with a fitting memorial to the village's best-known inhabitant, a colourful window depicting St. Francis, surrounded, as Gilbert White liked to be, by birds and beasts and flowers.

When The Wakes was in dire need of essential money for its maintenance and development, help was forthcoming from Robert Washington Oates, who made available an endowment for that purpose. In tribute to this most welcome generosity, the top floor of the house is devoted to the benefactor's family, and in particular to the brave Captain Lawrence Oates who was one of the five-man expedition to the South Pole, led by Captain Scott at the beginning of this century, which ended in tragedy in 1912 with the loss of all lives on the return journey.

It is the saddest room, a room of courage and enthusiasm which turned to paralysing disappointment, despair and death. For, after a gruelling journey of hardship and misfortune, with only the hope of achieving their goal to sustain them, they arrived to find the Norwegian flag already flying there. Captain Scott's daily log relates the long trek back, dogged still by disaster and ill-luck, and the sense of bitter futility where there should have been glorious triumph. Their equipment, by modern standards, was woefully inadequate; some of their pathetic trappings are there to see. It was Captain Oates who, weak and knowing that he could only be a hindrance to his already desperate companions, walked out into the blizzard, to die alone in the intolerable cold. But they all died. The last heart-breaking entry in the log reports " . . . it seems a pity but I can't seem to write any more . . . we will go on to the end of course, but the end cannot be far". Almost mercifully perhaps, it wasn't far. As I said, it is the saddest room.

Exploring seems to run in the family however, and Lawrence's uncle Frank Oates adventured far afield in the warmer climates of Africa and South America; another room is devoted to his exhibition.

A good many Hampshire folk will be content to spend their time exploring the more comfortable area of Abbotstone Down, a favourite spot for picnickers among thirty-two acres of grassland, thick woods, and views of the Itchen streams. One of the richest churches in the area belongs to Northington, a very grand building provided by the fourth Lord Ashburton, with an interior filled with gilded wrought iron, elaborate carved marble, and coloured windows.

Signposts pointing to "The Candovers" have intrigued strangers over the years, but they refer simply to the three villages of Preston Candover, Brown Candover and Chilton Candover, which succeed each other southward on the B3046 leading to Alresford.

Winchester Cathedral from the cloisters

Cathedral Gardens,
Winchester

Cheyney Court,
Winchester

St Cross, Winchester

Roman wall,
Silchester

The Vyne,
near Basingstoke

Tudor gallery,
The Vyne

Watercress beds in north Hampshire

The Old Mill, Langstone Harbour

East Meon Church

Sheep Street, Petersfield

Vineyard at Hambledon

Overleaf: Portsmouth Cathedral; Old Portsmouth

III

THE SOUTH-EAST

Alresford is mentioned in seventh-century records, and was an important place when Godfrey de Lucy was Bishop of Winchester five centuries later. The wool trade was at its peak then, and Alresford was its downland heart. Better still, the little Arle rose nearby and flowed into the Itchen which was a direct route to the sea nearly thirty miles away, at Southampton. Using his own money, and what engineering skill was available, the far-sighted bishop developed the village pond into a 200-acre reservoir, dammed it, and made the river navigable for the wool-laden barges, right through to the coast, with easy access to the Channel and foreign trading ports.

The pond has now shrunk to a fraction of its twelfth-century size, and fish and waterfowl breed there unhindered; but the bishop's causeway still takes traffic between Old and New Alresford.

Like other old towns, Alresford's history is one of fire and plague, poverty and prosperity. Its boomtime ended with the removal of the wool staple to Calais, but it revived as a cloth centre, with no less than four fulling-mills during the reign of Henry VIII. Later, coaches stopped there too, the Mail coach, travelling from the Bell and Crown Inn at Holborn to Poole, and stage coaches setting out from the Bell Savage at Ludgate Hill, or the Swan with Two Necks at Charing Cross, bound for Southampton.

The town is formed in a large T-shape, and in the aptly named Broad Street lived Mary Russell Mitford, author of several local novels, the best known of which is probably *Our Village*. At the age of ten, she won a fortune on a lottery ticket bought for her by her father, but he quickly took possession of it, and squandered the whole. It seems that Miss Mitford was well aware of her worth however, for she is recorded as stating that Alresford would be famous for two reasons, of which her birth was one. It would seem that she was right, for no feature on Alresford is written without mentioning her!

It is not often that the wife of a minister is better known than her husband, but so it is with Mary Sumner, whose foundation of the Mothers' Union has made her name familiar in all corners of the world where Christian communities flourish. Mary Sumner was the wife of Old Alresford's rector, and she held the first meeting of parish mothers at the red-brick church in 1876. Her memorial is there, together with that of naval hero Admiral Rodney, who built the great house next to the church.

Watercress is the renowned crop of the chalk streams, where the constantly fresh water springs provide a steady temperature of 51 degrees Fahrenheit, which is ideal for the crisp green plant. Almost anywhere in the area, flat beds of gravel on chalk are to be found, usually dried out in the early year, ready for the seeds or cuttings from older plants for the new season's crop. Watercress can be grown all the year round, but the plant requires maximum light to grow the longest, leafiest stems, so the main harvest is gathered between July and October. When the 'Beeching Axe' fell on country railways, Alresford lost its vital link with the retailers, and has now to rely on lorries to carry the produce to markets all over the country, for half of England's demand for watercress is produced in Hampshire. Railway enthusiasts being what they are, a 'Watercress Line Committee' was set up, and after many years of planning and saving, the three-mile length of railway line was purchased, and steam trains are running again in the summer months, showing tourists the picturesque route between Alresford and Ropley.

One of the county's best-known farms divides its interests between watercress and a dairy herd. John Mills came to Hampshire from Sussex in 1873, and was probably the first farmer to grow watercress there commercially, setting out his beds in the Bighton valley. At the turn of the century, the Mills family rented land nearby at Bishop's Sutton, and bought it later when the owner ran into financial difficulties.

In the 1920s, Mr Mills's sons started to build up a pedigree dairy herd of Shorthorns, which over a period of forty years won several show cups, including the coveted Southern Area

Gold Cup for the "best average for a Shorthorn cow over three years". Farming was their life, and the brothers were founder-directors of S.C.A.T.S. (Southern Counties Agricultural Trading Society), dealing in a comprehensive range of equipment from grain to tractors, and becoming well-known nationally in farming circles.

With his uncle, who is a 'sleeping partner', Peter Mills owns the farm now, great-grandson of the old man from Sussex, and he manages this 800 acres of Hampshire's prime agricultural land. Some of it is given over to cereal, mainly for domestic use, and 18 acres are retained to follow the family tradition of watercress-growing, making it the second largest producer in the county. The rest of the land is for the dairy herd, which has been changed over the years to the breed of British Friesians, 130 cows, each of which is expected to average a milk yield of 1200 gallons a year. Mr Mills believes deeply in the 'personal touch', and keeps mechanisation down to a necessary minimum. In the summer the herd is paddock grazed, but, as the year progresses they are brought inside to large, airy winter quarters, and separated into two groups, determined by their high or low milk yield, and for each group a different feeding pattern is required. Until Christmas, the cows will be fed with kale and hay and barley nuts, made from home-grown cereal mixed with a protein-concentrate, but after the new year, the kale is replaced with silage.

Calving is 'arranged' for the autumn and winter months, and the last tiny stragglers are born in middle March. It is hoped that every cow will calve each year, cow-calves joining the herd, and the young bullocks being sold for beef at eighteen months.

It is a busy and demanding life, but Peter Mills is happy with his lot. During a rare few days 'away from it all' on the other side of the world, a holiday-maker was heard to say that nothing could compare with strolling along that tropical beach. The young farmer did not agree. "Walking across my land on a spring morning beats that any time," he says contentedly.

And well he might. This central south-Hampshire land belongs very much to the River Itchen, whose lush valley starts near to Cheriton, with small tributaries flowing in from Chilton Candover in the north, and Bishop's Sutton in the

east, to meet at Ovington. Some of the county's prettiest
villages are here, and historic churches hide in quaint corners.
Tichborne's church of St Andrew must surely be unique,
housing as it does under one roof a place of worship for
Church of England and Roman Catholic alike.

Many are the stories that surround the ancient Tichborne
family, most of them too well known to repeat – the Tichborne Dole, the Tichborne Claimant and so on; but the most
poignant comes to light in the little Catholic chapel, where
memorials to the family fill much of the space. There is the
statue of a small boy, Richard Tichborne, who died in 1619
aged "one yeare six monthes and too daies". It is said that a
gypsy called at the house begging, and was turned away. In
her spite, she put a curse on the baby, that he would die by
drowning on the day she appointed. With the river so near,
the anxious parents took extra precautions on the fateful day,
and sent the boy out with his maids to the Downs, well away
from the water. But the servants were more attentive to their
own pursuits than to their charge; left to amuse himself, the
child leaned too far out of his baby-carriage, and it toppled
over. The cart-track was rough, and rain water had collected
in the ruts; as predicted, the baby drowned there.

Nowhere in this part of Hampshire is without memories of
the Civil War, and like Tichborne, nearby Cheriton was
much involved. The mounds that edge the village are said to
cover two thousand dead, killed in the battle of 1644, when,
anticipating an undisciplined Royalist charge down a narrow
lane, Waller's Roundheads were waiting, and cut the army
down in a most frightful carnage.

It is difficult to imagine a more peaceful village, with
attractive cottages grouped round the triangular green, ducks
always ready for tit-bits in the Itchen stream, and the square
tower of the church just beyond the rooftops.

The source of the River Itchen is a mile or so away on the
road to Kilmeston, where springs form a quiet pool by the
lane-side in wet seasons, starting off the journey that ends
nearly thirty miles away at the port of Southampton. Here, in
the same river, the world's largest liners have lain at anchor.
There is much of interest along its route.

When the Domesday Book was compiled by William's
men in 1086, there was an old house at Afintune; there is still

a house there, though not the same one, and now it is known as Avington House. Its frontage is vaguely reminiscent of The Vyne, of red brick with a white portico, and a view across a sheet of water. Part of the house is open to the public at limited times, but only a few rooms are shown, as the building is now divided into private flats.

For over a hundred years, until 1952, the house was in the possession of the Shelley family, having been bought by the poet's brother John, in 1848.

The Duke of Chandos lived there during Regency days, when the Prince was a regular visitor, often with his favourite companion, Mrs Fitzherbert. They liked to enjoy the peace of this country house, and to join with the villagers in their May Day celebrations, just as Charles II and his various ladies had done two centuries earlier. No doubt the Royal visits provided the residents with sufficient gossip to last them the year round.

The Marquess of Carnaervon was another owner, and his wife, Lady Margaret, had a great influence in the planning and superintending of the brick church whose square tower can be seen above the cedars of Lebanon edging the park. A grass path leads from the house to the north door of the church, which has often been quoted as 'one of the most perfect Georgian churches in the country'. It has a charm all its own, due presumably, to the love expended on it by the Marchioness. All the woodwork, including the high box pews and the elaborate pulpit are of a lovely dark mahogany, said to have been taken from a Spanish galleon after the Armada.

There is a story that St Augustine was associated with Avington at the end of the sixth century, when he came from Rome to convert the heathen English.

Across the curve of the river is the very old grey church of Itchen Abbas, and in the grounds lies the grave of a horse-thief, reputedly the last man to be hanged in England for that offence.

There are four Worthys in these parts, but the Ministry of Agriculture has made Martyr Worthy the best-known in farming circles by siting an Experimental Husbandry Farm there. This important centre, Bridgets, provides a vital service to agricultural progress, both in livestock and arable fields. The Ministry has a chain of thirteen such farms throughout

England and Wales, each having different conditions of soil, situation and weather. Bridgets stands at an altitude of 300 feet (91 m), and is one of the larger farms, with an area of 428 hectares on mainly chalk soil.

Detailed and extensive records are kept on experiments to determine the best crops to grow, which fertilisers to use, and how to cope with pests and diseases. Wheat, potatoes, rape, beans, maize and kale are all grown under controlled conditions, their handling and progress noted and compared, and then improved or discarded; the talk is of cereal cyst, eelworm and mildew; of nitrogen, potash, phosphate and lime, of drainage, silage and soil temperatures.

Animals play a large part in this scientific farming, with a pedigree herd of cows being studied for the results of feeding programmes, housing, breeding methods and milk yield. There is an Open Day each year, when the public are invited to visit the farm and ask questions of the experts, and an annual review is published, with the results of the year's findings. Old farming lore, at Bridgets, is a thing of the past; it all seems rather clinical and impersonal to a casual observer, but the service to agriculture is undeniable, and no doubt the ends justify the means.

By contrast, there is Ovington, the confluence of many streams, rural and natural, pleasant enough at any season, but a real delight in high summer, when the scent of meadow-sweet rises in almost overwhelming richness. The riverside walk is a naturalists' joy, with pink willow-herb and purple vetch, hemp-agrimony and loosestrife, huge marsh-thistles and bright yellow mimulus. There are voles and shrews, coots, moorhens, grebes and ducks, with so many birds singing overhead that identification of any one individual becomes a problem. The walk is a favourite with locals and visitors alike, and, caught at the right time, is one of the most beautiful spots in all Hampshire.

Beauworth is not far away, as pastoral a hamlet as any in the county, with pretty cottages grouped round a tiny old church, and half a mile away, the isolated Fox and Hounds, the village 'local'. High on the Downs, just off the A272, with only the sounds of rooks and sheep for company, this old inn has a special attraction for tourists. In a store-room behind the two cosy bars, is a well which has been dated as 1135, and above it, a three-hundred-year-old tread wheel for drawing the water. The wheel is a great hoop twelve feet in diameter, the rim about a yard wide being supported by sturdy spars from the central hub. The well was in daily use until the middle of this century, and a donkey was used to hoist the bucket from the 300-foot shaft, the 'walk' amounting to a time-and-energy-consuming half mile. Under normal conditions the well contains between twenty and thirty feet of water, but in the drought of 1976 the level subsided to only seven feet, which was not considered 'safe' for pure quality. The well was last used in that year, and village children were press-ganged into service for the half-mile tread, though without much difficulty, and were rewarded with that perennial favourite, a bag of crisps.

Mary New was born at the Fox and Hounds, which has been in her family for 112 years, and she and her husband Frank became licensees in 1963: since then visitors from all over the world have asked to see the wheel. But Frank New has made his mark in Hampshire in his own right; the tall, skilfully patterned brick chimneys on the cottages of Hursley, south-west of Winchester, are his work, and their craftsmanship is an important feature of the village.

Happily, the skills and interests of humankind are diverse. When John Knowles was taken, at the age of seven, to visit a zoo, he promptly informed his father that he was going to be an elephant-keeper when he grew up. He was never to achieve that particular ambition, but in 1972, he did open a 150-acre zoological park at Marwell, near the village of Owslebury. John Knowles is deeply concerned with the survival and conservation of animal species whose numbers in the wild are declining rapidly, mainly through man's indiscriminate take-over of their natural habitat.

The estate surrounds Marwell Hall, with its tall chimneys, and its history dating back to the 1300s, although the present house was largely rebuilt in 1815. It was the home of the turbulent Seymour family, and Henry Tudor, already twice married, did much of his courting of young Jane there. The Seymours were an ambitious clan, and it is said that there were great celebrations at Marwell when the chain of beacons were lit across the hills from London, giving the news that Anne Boleyn and her head were finally parted, leaving the ill-assorted lovers free to commence their own nuptials. Legend has it that the tragic Anne haunts the Yew Walk.

If that is so, I hope she does not mind the red pandas that sway in the tree-tops nearby, and is not alarmed by the raucous mating-call of the Sarus crane from the adjoining paddock, a noise calculated to frighten off any ghosts; perhaps not Anne though, for whatever her faults, she never lacked courage.

Only a small proportion of Marwell's animals come straight from the wild; most are born in the park, or exchanged with others from similar establishments to avoid too-close in-breeding. The park's owner is anxious to dispel the image of the Big White Hunter with pith helmet and rifle, capturing wild beasts for sport, or for short term exhibition and an early death in solitary confinement. The role of zoos has changed, he says, and Marwell is managed with sensitivity and affection; the welfare and contentment of the animals is the first priority, and their new homes are provided with thought and care, to re-create as closely as possible the conditions natural to them.

One of the park's biggest achievements is considered to be the Scimitar Horned Oryx, which has adapted well from its native desert-fringe, and an infant Addax, a small antelope, thought to be the first recorded birth in the United Kingdom in a hundred years. There are tigers from Sumatra and Siberia, flamingoes and jaguars from America, zebras, ostriches and giraffes from Africa, wallabies and emus from Australia, monkeys, porcupines and camels from Eurasia, and many more, though strangely for those early plans, no elephants! Many of the residents are recognisable only by the know-ledgeable, and perhaps the most famous rarity of all is a herd of wild horses, which, if they survive at all naturally, can only be found in the mountains of eastern Mongolia.

Running costs for an organisation such as Marwell are immense, in excess of £4,000 a week; food accounts for the largest single item, even though the home-farm provides all the hay and straw required. No Government subsidies are forthcoming to assist such projects, and in 1978, John Knowles took the astute step of making Marwell into a charitable trust. Although the park is primarily a breeding sanctuary, the public are encouraged to visit the grounds; yet incredibly, visitors have been known to violate this welcome and ruin years of devoted care by smashing precious eggs, and hurling missiles at timid creatures. Not so long ago, the new-born foal of a wild horse – one of the rarest animals in the world – was killed when the herd was stoned by hooligans; and almost unbelievably, there is the tale of boys feeding a delightful pair of friendly otters with lighted cigarette ends ...!

Happily, the majority of visitors are interested, and take pleasure in what is going on. Marwell's staff will not quickly forget the flood of world-wide sympathy that deluged the park in September 1977, when Victor the giraffe slipped and fell, leaving himself straddled, long legs akimbo, flat, uncomfortable and unable to raise himself. The world's Press followed his progress, and the whole world seemed saddened when despite unceasing efforts to help him, Victor died. No one mourned more than John Knowles. One day, as he was preparing to leave for Helsinki to bring back a snow leopard, I asked him if he still felt excited at the prospect of a new arrival at the park. "You must," he said, "or it's time to retire. If the day comes when you are not gladdened by a birth – or saddened by a death – then it's time to go." For him, that day is not imminent, it seems.

Between Marwell and the A33 close to Otterbourne, lies the grey pile of Brambridge House, where George IV is said to have married Mrs Fitzherbert, the lady who has been described as "his only love". But restrictive legislation governed such vital affairs as Royal marriages, and the contract was not considered to be legally binding; the king later married Caroline of Brunswick, who to put it mildly, he did not like, but continued to visit his favourite at Brambridge, remembering her with deep affection till his death.

At Otterbourne, Charlotte Yonge wrote about the countryside she observed so closely, and also completed a number of charming and innocent novels. A firm friend of neighbouring rector John Keble and his wife, Charlotte was herself much interested in church matters; she taught bible subjects in the day and Sunday school near her home, and donated the income from her books to missions abroad, financing a schooner and buildings for the missionaries' use, as well as spending large sums on the new church being built beside the main road, where she is remembered by a cross over the chancel rails.

Nearby too, is the elegant Cranbury Hall, whose one-time owner, Lee Dummer, sought to possess Winchester's Butter Cross. Sir Isaac Newton was a regular visitor to the house when his friend John Conduitt lived there.

What the Army did for Aldershot, the London and South Western Railway has done for Eastleigh, turning a long-established rural hamlet between Winchester and Southampton into a flourishing town. The geometric criss-crossing roads were unimaginatively edged with red-brick houses, in which lived the families of men employed in the Carriage and Wagon Works that had been moved from London's Nine Elms to Hampshire at the end of the nineteenth century. The vast marshalling yards are still there, with the station on the main line from Waterloo to the west, and the image of 'railway town' has persisted since its Victorian establishment. It is an image that today's planners are striving to eradicate and, slowly, they are succeeding. In 1977, the town won a national competition for environmental improvement, and more changes are on the drawing-board. Progress there must be, but I am sorry that the old Town Hall is now obsolete, a dignified building of mellow brick, with a clock under a cupola; a building bright with hanging-baskets and window-boxes of seasonal flowers and only a stone's throw from the park and the bandstand. It is all an age away from the blinding glass walls of the borough's new civic headquarters, which is what, of course, they set out to achieve!

In 1974, the athlete Mary Peters opened Eastleigh's new sports complex in the 120-acre Fleming Park. It caters for both indoor and outdoor activities, from swimming, squash and badminton, to yoga, archery, golf and football, and even includes a sauna, solarium and weight-training unit.

Industry is thriving too; huge drums of high-voltage power-cable, used all over the world, are made at Pirelli-General; 'Mr Kipling' bakes his cakes and bread there, and Hillspan erect large pre-fabricated farms and industrial build-ings – all this and a large working estate on the eastern edge of the town. The first hypermarket to be built south of the Thames is sited near Eastleigh, and so is Hampshire's only commercial airport. Both Southampton and Eastleigh laid claim to its title, and the controversy was diplomatically settled by calling it Southampton (Eastleigh) Airport. Passengers and freight are carried to and from all corners of the British Isles, to the Channel Islands and to Europe by regular scheduled air-lines, and an air-taxi is also available.

The suburbs of the town have spread in all directions, but particularly to the east, where the road crosses the Itchen, and gets itself involved with the muddy roadworks of the new M27 link.

The winding lanes through agricultural country lead to Bishops Waltham, at the head of the stream which becomes the Hamble River. Bishops Waltham was one of the main residences of the bishops of Winchester; Henri de Blois began to build a castle there in 1136, and it was much enlarged by William of Wykeham, who liked to spend much of his time at this extensive palace, dying here in 1404. Only the tower and parts of the old grey walls are left, the rest is one of the largest ruins in the south.

Bishops Waltham is a pleasant town, overlooked by a large flint church reached by a narrow sloping street between houses of character, on whose walls last year's birds' nests are exposed in winter amongst the leafless tangle of honeysuckle and wistaria.

I do not know how it is, but as I come to each area, I think of it as "one of the most beautiful in the county". I suppose the simple answer is, that to a Hampshire Hog, all parts of the county *are* beautiful. Certainly the Meon Valley, running from the high chalk downs to the river-mouth at Stubbington, is very lovely, with distant views from the ridges of Corhampton and Old Winchester Hill, and Catherington, farther south, and a spattering of churches and villages, some famed for their great age, others for their scenery.

West Meon, close beside the young river, in whose church grounds lie the remains of Thomas Lord, founder of Lords Cricket Ground; he died in the village after retiring to farm there; Corhampton, on the edge of the downs, with possibly the oldest church in Hampshire, a Saxon building with a sundial; Droxford, where our old angling friend Izaak Walton spent many happy hours in his later life by the Meon, and where his daughter, Anne, married the rector of the village.

One of the larger communities, built around the market square, is Wickham, where England's great Chancellor William was born in 1324. A fascinating old place, Wickham, with some elegant Georgian frontages, and behind them, opposite the mill once powered by the Meon stream that still trickles by, some old timbered cottages. Roadsters received short shrift here it seems, for a cottage wall bears the stern warning "Notice is Hereby Given that all Vagrants Found in or near This Place will be apprehended and Punished with the Utmost Severity the Law will Permit. By Order of the Magistrates."

Farther north, rising high above the valley, near the source of the River Meon, is the chevron-spire of East Meon's lovely church. It is set high on a green slope, surrounded by limes and conifers, and a mass of daffodils in springtime. The hill behind it rises higher yet. One of Hampshire's four Tournai marble fonts is at East Meon, hewn from one solid block and decorated with scenes from the story of the Creation. The church has many treasures, including a Jacobean pulpit of 1706, which belonged to a church in the parish of the Tower of London. The pulpit was brought to East Meon when the church was dismantled, by the vicar, who then accustomed himself to house-martins instead of London sparrows as he served his new country parish. The martins nest there still, sure of a welcome, for as today's vicar says in true Christian spirit, "They make a mess, but we love to have them."

Old Winchester Hill watches benignly over the valley, 140 acres of land supported by the Nature Conservancy Council. Men of the Iron Age knew these chalk hills, and no doubt their sheep grazed the short succulent grass, even as do the sheep of the twentieth century. Ramparts of their old community can be traced in the soil, and a Nature Trail has been arranged for visitors. In the summer, Old Winchester Hill is a favourite spot, and even in winter it is unusual to be entirely alone there, for someone always comes along to walk their dog, to eat their packed lunch, or just to look at the patchwork views, the tower of Warnford church, and at the specks of aircraft with tails of smoke from their jet-engines, leaving Heathrow way, way in the distance.

It is known that the art of vine cultivation was brought to Britain by the Romans, but the seed for the foundation of Hampshire's best-known vineyard was sown in France during the First World War. In the autumn of 1917, English soldiers found themselves sharing a cold and muddy trench with

French comrades, and the only difference in their circumstances was that the French army was issued with a wine ration. They were good enough to share this morale-booster with the less fortunate troops, and thus began what one of those grateful soldiers calls 'a rewarding romance with wine'.

That soldier of long ago is now Major-General Sir Guy Salisbury-Jones, G.C.V.O., C.M.G., C.B.E., M.C., and when he ended a long and distinguished military career in 1949, he settled at Mill Down at Hambledon, although the following ten years were spent mostly in London in his new capacity as Marshal of the Diplomatic Corps. The slopes around his Hampshire home spread southwards – on a clear day you can see the Isle of Wight – and receive a generous share of the day's sunshine. In 1952, it was suggested that the land would be eminently suitable for siting a vineyard, and much thought was given to the project, so near to Sir Guy's heart. So, with his gardener, the enthusiast set out for the advice of friends in Burgundy. His visit coincided with a lavish banquet in the neighbourhood, and Sir Guy always says, with a distinct twinkle in his eye, that it was due to the elevating influence of this Burgundian hospitality that he returned to England the proud, if rather doubtful, owner of 4,000 vines. But he has never looked back.

Hambledon's downland soil is similar to that of the Champagne area of north-east France, and the resulting dry white wine has been likened by the experts to a still Champagne; advice and co-operation from the House of Pol Roger, producers of Sir Winston Churchill's favourite Champagne, has been of great value at Hambledon.

Sir Guy's original vines were mostly Seyval, grafted for 'health reasons' on to American rootstock, but since 1975 the number of superior Chardonnay, Pinot Meunier and Pinot Noir has been increased. The vineyard consists of nearly five acres, about the same size as that of Romanée Conti in Burgundy, reputedly "the most precious vineyard in the world".

The making of Hambledon Wine is a year-round industry. Now in his middle-eighties, Sir Guy necessarily leaves much of the heavier work to his manager and staff, but he is still actively involved in his business, and Lady Salisbury-Jones helps with the paper-work. Maintenance and clearance fill the

winter months; early frosts and summer hailstorms are an
anxiety, and rabbits too, but the greatest enemy (apart from
an unsympathetic Excise system) is the blackbird, and the
distribution of wide-spread all-over netting has become a
yearly chore.

The vines flower at the beginning of July, and it is estimated that a hundred days will elapse before the harvest.
Then all available local help comes to gather the smooth
grapes into individual trugs, from which they are loaded into
large baskets and humped to the wine-making house. The
grapes are pulped, pressed, left first to settle and then to
ferment with sugar and a special yeast; for three months the
wine is allowed to mature before bottling. Each bottle (an
average of 8,000 per season) is hand-corked, and they are taken
to the cellar, but labels are not affixed until the bottle is
purchased. Most of the wine is sold on the premises to tourists
who are allowed to visit from time to time, but much is sent
abroad. The main branch of Peter Dominic in London, and
their branches at Winchester, Southampton and Chichester
stock bottles, and Hambledon supplies the National Theatre.
The wine is also served at Scott's Restaurant in London's
Mount Street. I am not a connoisseur of wine, but I know
what I like; and I like Hambledon.

The elegant label on the bottle depicts the scene for which
Hambledon has been famous for two hundred years, the
curved bat and two-legged wicket of early cricketing days.
From the east window of Sir Guy's house on the top of Mill
Down, the undulating green rolls away to Broad Halfpenny
Down, home ground of the renowned Hambledon team, who
played England's finest cricket at the end of the eighteenth
century. Hambledon has variously been called the birthplace
and the cradle of cricket, both of which claims are sharply
denied by the purists. But the skill of the players, and the
tremendous spirit of the team at that time, made it the best
known team in all England. A great granite monument in a
corner of the ground commemorates those glorious days, when
at the end of the game the teams gathered at the Bat and Ball
across the lane, its landlord himself a notable bowler, to wet
their whistles and to sing of their successes, for the Hambledon
men loved to sing.

John Nyren, son of one of the village's heroes, wrote a most evocative and entertaining book★ on his boyhood memories of the game, and of the men who formed the nucleus of those grand days of the 1770s. "There was high feasting held on Broad Halfpenny during the solemnity of one of our grand matches. Oh! it was a heart-stirring sight to witness the multitude forming a complete and dense circle round that noble green. Half the county would be present, and all their hearts with us – Little Hambledon, pitted against all England, was a proud thought for the Hampshire men. Defeat was glory in such a struggle – Victory, indeed, made us only 'a little lower than the angels'. How those fine brawn-faced fellows of farmers would drink to our success! And then what stuff they had to drink . . . . How strongly are all those scenes, of fifty years by-gone, painted in my memory! – and the smell of that ale comes upon me as freshly as the new May flowers." True, honest, sporting Englishmen of yester-year, playing for no other reason than for joy of the game. The book is a breath of pure fresh air, and I recommend it to cricketers and non-cricketers alike.

Crowds flocked again to Broad Halfpenny in the summer of 1977, when a bicentenary match was staged between today's Hambledon men, a small village side now, and the M.C.C., which, diplomatically, was drawn. The Down, in as rural a corner of Hampshire as you can find, is a splendid, if rather irregular place for a cricket pitch, high on the crest of the downs, with superb views of pasture, crops and woodland, the ground slightly rounded, giving the game an extra bite (!), and edged with a shady grove of beeches were spectators sit in their cars, or in striped garden chairs with picnic hampers at their feet. And still, the red-tiled Bat and Ball takes care of that after-match thirst.

Nowadays, the ground is used mainly by the team from H.M.S. *Mercury*, a naval establishment eighteen miles inland from Portsmouth. The 'ship' was formerly the private residence Leydene House, but was occupied by the Royal Navy during the war. H.M.S. *Mercury* is the navy's main signal school, instructing some five hundred officers and ratings at any one time in the skills of Communications and Electronic Warfare.

This is the edge of the area known as Little Switzerland, with its high green hills and deep valleys, and steep, white-

★ *Cricketers of my Time.*

faced escarpments. The highest 'peak' of them all is Butser, at 888 feet, the highest point in Hampshire. The views – on a clear day – are magnificent. A country park of nearly 1,400 acres surrounding Butser Hill was opened by Her Majesty the Queen in August 1976, and it was on Butser that the only Hampshire beacon in the 'chain of bonfires' lit throughout the Commonwealth to mark the Queen's Silver Jubilee in 1977, was sited. I am not sure whether managing the land as a park has been a good idea or not; somehow, the 'wildness' and naturalness – the very qualities the organisers wished to conserve, seem to have evaporated in some mysterious way.

No one knows with any certainty just how long man has inhabited these hills; certainly for thousands of years travellers roamed along the ancient trackways, farmers have tilled the scant soil, and craftsmen have fashioned their tools and ornaments. The fine beech trees provided excellent building timber, and the iron-furnaces of the Weald were fired by their charcoal; the plentiful flint in the soil was also used for building and road-making, and even for cumbersome old pistols. The country park managers are trying to re-create these old industries and crafts, which includes the building of an Iron Age homestead, a roundhouse with conical thatched roof, old English game fowl, Dexter cattle and Soay sheep, a loom with upright warpweight, and a clay pit for cooking. There is so much literature printed about the site, which should be interesting, but I find that I am sadly put off by talk of 'guided walks' and 'an audio-visual theatre', and being told that 'the energetic can hire boots and skies', for grass-skiing which, with hang-gliding, is a sport for which Butser is eminently suitable. No doubt the park is a wonderful public amenity, but I wish they had left it alone.

The steep verges winding through the chalk hill-passes are thick in July with ox-eye daisies, tall thistles, and masses of blue flowers that I have never been able to identify, although they *look* like purple bugloss. It makes a lovely vista, one that is familiar to the veteran actor, Sir Alec Guinness, who made his home on the outskirts of Petersfield twenty-five years ago, in a house designed by his brother-in-law. His twelve-acre property overlooks these ever-changing and never-changing hills; it is no wonder that this busy man has found peace and contentment there.

Petersfield is the only town of any size in the area, and it has a comfortable and unhurried atmosphere wholly in keeping with its surroundings. Near to the Sussex border, the old community was founded on a sandy waste at the west end of the Weald, at the intersection of ancient trackways, between 1150 and 1175, by William, Earl of Gloucester. Like other southern towns, Petersfield's medieval prosperity depended largely on wool, and the villagers carried on an important cloth industry from their homes. In due course, leather-tanning became a useful source of income, with hop-growing and brewing filling many a worker's pocket. With the introduction of the coach service, Petersfield developed into a busy posting-centre; in 1830 as many as thirty coaches a day stopped in the town for the refreshment of passengers and a change of horses. All that came to an end when the Portsmouth to London railway line was opened.

A statue of William III dominates the Square, erected in 1753 and sculpted in lead by John Cheere, out of £500 provided for the purpose in the will of Sir William Jolliffe, a member of one of the town's leading families at that time. The people cannot have cared much for it, for the statue fell into sad disrepair, and was only restored this century, being unveiled with much festivity, in 1913.

The church of St Peter stands directly behind the monument. It too has been restored, but some of the original twelfth-century features are still evident, including the unusual chancel arch. John Small, one of the old Hambledon team (and maker of their cricket balls) was buried in the graveyard in 1826, after reaching the grand old age of 89.

Petersfield Heath, where flint implements of Mesolithic man dating back to 5000 BC have been found, has become one of the town's best rural amenities. For seven hundred years, a Heath Fair has been held on the sixty-nine-acre site on 6th October; it was originally a horse fair, but like most events of this kind, is now more of a stalls and roundabouts affair.

Beside the north-east road out of the town, Churcher's College was founded in 1722, by Richard Churcher, an East India merchant. The establishment was for the education of twelve locals boys, whose curriculum was to include navigation, with the intention that they should afterwards become apprenticed to Masters of ships of the East India Company. The boys wore long blue coats, and their hats were decorated with a pewter badge bearing the Company's coat of arms. The original building has now become Council Offices, and the present school, which has around 450 pupils, dates from 1881.

Much better known is the school founded by John Haden Badley, a remarkable man who died in 1967 at the age of 102. Mr Badley had revolutionary ideas about education, and started his own tiny school in 1893 at a Sussex house called Bedales. He believed in a freedom of thought and expression which, though we take it for granted today, was unheard of in the strict Victorian era of "spare the rod and spoil the child". He believed in balanced, all-round learning, the co-education of girls and boys, and a less inhibited relationship between teacher and pupil.

In 1900, the school moved to Hampshire, and settled in the Steep area just north of Petersfield, where Bedales flourishes today in its 150-acre estate. The number of pupils has risen steadily from the original three of the first term, to in excess of five hundred. Ages range from 3½ to 18 years, with the majority of the older pupils being boarders.

Great emphasis is placed on an adult approach to education, and the children are encouraged to be responsible for themselves. Proper standards in academic subjects are required, but other talents are also developed, whether they be directed into sport, music, science or art. Bedales claims an 80 per cent 'pass' rate at higher G.C.E. levels, and sends about thirty entrants to university places in any one year.

The list of Old Bedalians who have found success in their chosen fields is impressive, and includes such familiar names as Sir Malcolm MacDonald, John Wyndham, George Sanders and Joanna Dunham; this method of education was chosen for the children of Princess Margaret and Lord Snowdon.

Ex-pupils and staff have a deep affection and admiration for John Haden Badley. One said that he was a "whole person", and that he had a love of beauty, of goodness and of truth, with a hatred of cruelty and injustice. Bedales children do not wear a uniform, but as a resident of Petersfield said to me, "You can always tell a Bedales person in the town". It was said kindly, and in these days when individual freedom is so abused, that is nice to know; perhaps the wisdom of its founder has something to do with it.

It was not so many years ago, that the eastern strip of the county was one large expanse of forest land, Alice Holt, Woolmer Forest, Liss Forest, Forest of Bere, and various other tracts of woodland. Some remnants of these great stretches remain, but much has been cleared, some to make warships for Nelson's navy, some by modern governments. The Army occupies 5,000 acres of sandy heathland that was once Woolmer Forest, and which, since the turn of the century, has become Borden. The camp is a training ground, with extensive rifle-ranges which are used by several military units, and sometimes by other branches of the Armed Forces. A civilian population followed the setting up of the camp, and the village of Bordon was born.

Another camp built at the same time was Longmoor, among the pinewoods east of the A325 road from Petersfield to Farnham; until 1969, the unit trained soldiers in railway engineering and track-laying, vital skills for desolate, outlying areas in which the army might find itself, but such knowledge seems to be no longer required, for the unit has been disbanded. Film companies will miss the private stretch of railway track, for many comedies, dramas and thrillers had their train sequences made at Longmoor.

The winding roads south to the coast are spectacular, steep and beech-lined, a grotto of fresh green in spring, and a majestic wonderland of russet in October. As you start to smell the sea, the land flattens, and the trees are left behind.

You can go no further south or east in Hampshire than Emsworth, tucked away in the corner at the mouth of the little River Ems, which flows from Sussex and forms the county border. Medieval Emsworth was a busy harbour, exporting the all-important wool to France, and receiving continental merchandise in exchange. But the river-mouth opening into Chichester Harbour silted up, the death-knell of so many once-busy ports; now at low-tide, oyster-catchers and plovers delve into the salty mud for titbits, and small pleasure-craft lie high and dry. The oyster-beds and the brewery coasters are gone; the tidal-mill has 'gone electric', and the mill-pond is a bathing pool. Round the Square, old shops dating from 1750 are gathered, and smart Georgian streets recall the bustle of long-ago trade. The harbour is lined with expensive houses which face the road, their back gardens sloping down to the water's edge.

Hampshire's most easterly island of Hayling lies betwen the two harbours of Chichester and Langstone. A holiday island with an equable climate, Hayling covers ten flat square miles, shaped like an upside-down 'T', and just four miles long from north to south. The narrow toll-bridge connecting it to the mainland, although adequate for many years of local traffic, became a bane to impatient motorists, who fumed when most of their sunny days of leisure, due to be enjoyed at the seaside, were spent instead in a long, hot queue of simmering motor-cars. Authority took pity on the holiday-maker – whose custom it was in danger of losing – and in 1956 a wide new bridge was opened.

The northern strip of the island, dissected by narrow, bending roads, is largely given over to market-gardening and greenhouse-culture, while the south, with its long stretches of beach, much of it sandy, is the holiday haven. South Hayling is equipped with a funfair and all the trappings expected by holiday-makers, but the commerce of the tourist-trade has not yet ruined this pleasant area. The safe beaches are backed by dunes covered by, coarse, tussocky grass which are ideal for picnics, providing you watch out for gorse and thistles! I am told that the blue-flowered sea-holly, becoming quite a rarity nowadays, grows there too, but I have not been lucky enough to find any for myself; certainly campion grows taller on Hayling than I have seen it anywhere else, straggling head-high in places.

Both of Hayling's two churches are a joy, St Mary's in the south, and St Peter's in the north, both very old, and both with interesting features of architecture and history. St Mary's is large and light, and has that precious 'cared for' feeling. Mostly early English, it has a square centre tower beneath a slender, shingled spire, and in its grounds are kept the old village stocks and whipping-post, a reminder of days when the lawless were dealt with in summary, if rather savage, fashion.

St Peter's is the older of the two, built in 1140 on irregular granite boulders. Typically Norman, it is simply designed, with traditionally massive pillars and roof timbers. Its trio of bells, one dating from about 1350, are reputed to be the oldest in England, and hang from original wooden axles and half-wheels.

Woods clothe the north-east corner of the island, but the western coast is flat and marshy, and you can stand on the mudflats when the tide is flowing, and watch the frilled water-line edging perceptibly in, covering the algae and lifting the seaweed and pieces of cuttle-fish.

Over on the northern mainland, a tall turret of pale red brick, with a small segment of wall, is all that remains of the fortified house at Warblington, built between 1513 and 1526, which was the home of Margaret, Countess of Salisbury, who acted as governess to Princess Mary, daughter of Henry VIII and Catherine, his first wife. Margaret was the last of the Plantagenet nobles, and had a troubled life which ended with her execution at the Tower.

The flint-walled church of Thomas à Becket has an unusual triangular-shaped wall at the west end, supporting a steep-sided roof. In past years, Warblington's graveyard attracted the macabre trade of body-snatching, and in two corners of the grounds, a square hut of brick and stone remains, where the men who had the job of guarding the graves waited.

Langstone Harbour is arguably the south's most important winter stop-over for migrants from the Arctic and Siberia, and Farlington Marshes, in the sheltered north-west curve have been developed as a nature-reserve of some 280 acres for this vital purpose. There is much to interest the botanist, but it is the bird-watcher who is most in his element. In October, the first Brent Geese start to arrive from northern Russia, swarming in their thousands, to lodge for six months or so; they are soon joined by divers, mergansers, shovelers and widgeon which feed on the plentiful supply of shore-crabs, small fish and molluscs provided by the sea-lapped salt-marshes. The bay also supports a large variety of residents – curlews, godwits, plovers, oyster-catchers, turnstones, and many other waders; with such an abundance of birds and also flowers both common and rare, the naturalist cannot but be happy at Farlington. The tidal mill on the shore-line attracts artists to this picturesque place, but in past years, it was the smugglers who were attracted to the fifteenth-century Royal Oak nearby.

Directly across the harbour lies the other of the two islands, Portsea, with the sprawl of Cosham, Hilsea, Fratton and Eastney, suburbs that form the east-side of the great town-complex of Portsmouth.

IV

PORTSMOUTH

I think that the nicest way to approach Portsmouth is from the sea, sailing round the southern coast past Southsea Castle, and through the narrow harbour-mouth, Gosport on the left, and on the right the old fortifications that line the Point, great bulwarks against invasion from the French, although I confess that I find them less impressive from the seaward side than from the land. But there is a sense of history in viewing them as mariners have viewed them since the Middle Ages, coming and going from this busy port. And there is so much to see, and later to visit and explore – the ruins of the Garrison Church, wrecked by German bombers in the Second World War, the cupola-top of the cathedral, Quebec House on the shore-line, and all the haunts of Old Portsmouth, while farther on, the great mass of rigging rises above H.M.S. *Victory*'s brown and ochre bulk, set amidst the business-like grey ships of the Royal Navy.

To many people, the name of Portsmouth is synonymous with the Navy, and means only the dockyard and, inevitably, sailors. For many years that might have been a true impression, but times are changing. The Navy is still an integral part of the city and a major employee, but with reductions in sea-defence and the economic uncertainties that have bedevilled the 1970s, Portsmouth is wisely diversifying its interests.

Most of the city is contained on the flat Portsea Island, surrounded by the waters of Langstone and Portsmouth Harbours, an island by only a few feet of salt water when the lowest tide laps the northern edge; in addition, the City Council governs a strip along the mainland, from Bedhampton in the east, across Portsdown Hill to Portchester.

Although records show that Portsmouth existed long before 900, it was not of sufficient size to warrant a mention in the Domesday Book. But the town grew rapidly after the arrival

71

of the Normans, and saw much royal coming and going, for easy access to territories in northern France was a necessity. Richard I used the little port so often that he had a house built there, living in it while attending to the business of fitting out his fleet for the Crusade. To Portsmouth he returned after his imprisonment in Austria, and from there he plotted his revenge. He granted a charter to the town in 1194.

With a narrow entrance to a large natural harbour, and the sheltered and strategically safe anchorage of Spithead on its coastal doorstep, Portsmouth's role as a centre for naval activity was assured and has never faltered. The old town grew around Portsmouth Point, the south-west corner of the island, facing across the harbour entrance to Gosport, and defended from enemies by sturdy stone bastions.

The Round Tower, earliest of them all, was started around 1418, and today's bathers picnic and paddle between Point Battery and Sally Port, and the Square Tower. This great block of a building has had a varied career; having started as a defensive structure against the more destructive new weapons of war, it became, a hundred or so years later, a store for powder and shot. Governor George Goring, a Royalist colonel in the Civil War, haggled over the terms of surrender by threatening to set fire to the magazine and blow up the town. In the late 1700s, the cool interior was used to store meat for re-victualling naval ships calling between engagements for supplies and, in 1812, a semaphore signal-station on the roof formed one of a chain of fifteen sited between Portsmouth and London, enabling vital news to take less than ten minutes to reach the capital.

The morning sun glints on the gilded head and shoulders of a bust of Charles I, set in a circular recess of the tower's north wall, and presented by the king to Portsmouth in 1635. The inscription beneath informed his people that "After his travels through all France into Spain, and having passed very many dangers both by sea and land, he arrived here 5th day of October, 1623".

The Saluting Platform from which ceremonial gun salutes are fired, adjoins the Square Tower, and is still in use when occasion demands, as in 1977 when the Queen paid her Jubilee visit to the city.

Behind these old walls assembled the convicts who were to

be the first unwilling settlers of Australia, bound for Botany Bay in 1787.

This corner of Old Portsmouth is full of character, with narrow, cobbled streets edged by a jumble of tall houses with projecting upper storeys. A constant bustle of tugs and coasters, ferries and yachts moves in and out of the old Camber Dock, a deep inlet that curves among the wharves and warehouses, and a nest of old ale-houses that have served thirsty seamen for many a year. The Lone Yachtsman, with a Lively Lady Bar, was named in honour of Sir Alec Rose, who kept his yacht in the harbour, while the Still and West Country House has been serving suitable stimulants since 1700. Rows of wooden benches enable customers to sit in the garden on fine days, and take full advantage of the wide view across the harbour, even to the brick forts on the chalk ridge that rims the city.

Immediately on the right is H.M.S. *Vernon,* a shore establishment concerning itself with torpedoes and Sonar equipment; beyond spreads the dockyard, with the sky-raking masts and distinctive heavy rigging of H.M.S. *Victory* high above the grey roofs.

Anyone who fancies himself as an old seadog, strutting over the deck of a man o' war at a time when sailors really were sailors, can indulge himself to the full aboard this splendid ship, imagining the old timbers creaking beneath might sails billowing in the salty breeze, and the rows of cannons firing broadside after broadside at England's enemies.

It will all be in the mind though, for the old lady is safe in dry dock now, and greatly restored; indeed, there is little left of the original fabric, but it remains identical in every detail to its condition in the battling days of George III's navy; and visitors can tour this fine piece of history (free of charge) under naval escort.

But what a hard life it was. A crew of more than 800 slept in hammocks slung eighteen inches apart, and were fed with stew and stale biscuits from a tiny galley not much bigger than an average-sized domestic kitchen. Some of the crew were lads of eight or nine, 'powder monkeys' who climbed nimbly between the decks to feed the cannons at the height of the battle; many were apprentices and farm-boys, snatched by the press-gangs on their weary way home after a day's toil.

Discipline was harsh, disease rife, and battle-wounds horrific, as were the surgical instruments for dealing with them. Many men were needed to handle the huge ship's-wheel in heavy seas, and it took seven great anchors to steady the vessel.

Built at Chatham in 1759, the *Victory* saw much active service, and for six years, until his death from a sniper's bullet at Trafalgar, was the flagship of the incomparable Horatio Nelson. The tales that the sailor-guides tell are entirely absorbing, facts and figures related as they are to the great ship beneath your feet; tales of a way of life that can scarcely be imagined in these coddled days, of glory and bravery, hardship and brutality. Anyone who visits Portsmouth, and fails to see H.M.S. *Victory*, misses a fascinating and vital slice of English history.

One of the houses beside the hard at Portsmouth Point that Nelson would have known well by sight, is the white-timbered Quebec House, built in 1754 as a Bathing House where General Wolfe's body was brought home after the Battle of Quebec. The house gained notoriety in May 1845, when a captain in the Dragoons was shot dead in a duel with a Royal Marine, the last man (officially) to die in England from this very basic way of settling a squabble.

John Dickens, a pay-clerk in the Navy Pay Office would have known these streets of Old Portsmouth too, although his son was to be more familiar with the tenements of London. But Charles Dickens was born here, in Portsmouth, on 7th February 1812, in a smart terraced house near the docks. His parents habitually lived beyond their means, and the extra expense of the baby obliged them to move to smaller accommodation. Financial matters did not improve however, and when Charles was only two years old, he was taken with his parents to London, destined for a spell in a Debtors' Prison.

When, in his middle life, the famous novelist visited Portsmouth to give readings of his work, he strolled along the street of his birth, and identified the house where he was born. Now it stands as 393 Commercial Road, and has been restored as a museum, furnished and decorated in the fashion of the early nineteenth century, and even containing a few of Dickens's own possessions.

Not all Portsmouth's buildings were lucky enough to survive the relentless bombing raids of the 1940s. The Garrison

Church on the sea-front was left in ruins, and remains so to
this day, open to the sky, except for the chancel, which by
some miracle, escaped. Before this altar, in 1662, stood Charles
II and Catherine at their wedding, although the flippant king
had kept his bride, newly arrived from Braganza, kicking her
heels for several days, despite the much-needed dowry of
£300,000 she brought with her.

Like Winchester's St Cross, this old 'God's House' was
intended at the beginning of the thirteenth century for the
succour of the poor, the sick and the wayfarer, and was so
used for some time. Later, the town's military governor lived
in the buildings, and it became known as Government House;
the green beside the chapel is still called Governor's Green, and
a fair used to be held there, but complaints were received
about the bawdy 'goings on', and the fair was stopped.

The cathedral has suffered too from the wars, and like
Portsmouth itself, shows a marked contrast between the old
and the new, which, ecclesiastically at least, blend pleasingly
together. The see of Portsmouth was created in 1927, and the
town's mother church of St Thomas à Becket, the oldest in
the town, was chosen to be the cathedral. The building is not
in the traditional style, having a central tower over which has
been raised a cupola-top; the main entrance from the High
Street takes worshippers into the 'new' end, spacious and clear
cut, while the old parts date from the last quarter of the
twelfth century. I think it was Robert Louis Stevenson who
remarked that mankind was never so happily inspired as when
making a cathedral; there is little inspiration at Portsmouth,
but it is imposing, its lines dignified, and its interior a place of
peace. It takes time for a cathedral's character to form, and
fifty interrupted years are not long enough.

Just along the road lived John Pounds, a name not familiar
to people outside Portsmouth; he is one of the unsung bene-
factors who made so much difference to the lives of neighbourhood ragamuffins. A cobbler, a cripple and a poor man,
this good-hearted soul opened the door of his tiny home to
the ragged children of Portsmouth, of whom, as in most cities
at that time, there were many. There he instructed them in
the elementary education they would not otherwise have
known, seeing also that none wanted for food or for clothing.
John Pounds is remembered still in a little sanctuary off the

High Street, where the weary can take the weight from their feet and recover themselves quietly in this small garden away from the bustle of town. As unobtrusive as the man himself, I think that if he could have chosen his own memorial, he would not have been better pleased.

On the other side of the road lodged a character as flamboyant as John Pounds was modest, George Villiers, Duke of Buckingham, boyhood friend and partner in many a mischief of Charles II. There too, he died, murdered in his host's hallway, stabbed by a soldier who nursed a grievance against him. John Felton was the killer, and never denied it, having bought a knife especially and come from London for that sole purpose; he was hanged, and his body taken from the gallows of Tyburn, and hung in chains on Southsea Common.

That was a long time ago, and in place of the gruesome gibbet, there is a statue of that extraordinary man, Nelson, so small, so fragile, and yet with so magnetic a personality, and so courageous a heart. Here he stands on a high stone plinth, overlooking the beach from which in 1805 he joined the fine old *Victory* for the conflict of Trafalgar, from which he did not return. Portsmouth is full of nostalgia for the naval hero who knew the town so well, and a tall obelisk stands high above the island on Portsdown Hill, a tribute to the affection and respect in which he was held by his men, for each of the sailors who fought with him in his last action contributed from their meagre pay for the erection of the monument "to perpetuate his triumph and their regret", a continuing landmark and memorial.

Southsea beach still attracts sailors, and it was from there on the 16th July 1967 that a local shopkeeper sailed down the Solent in his 36-foot yacht, waved off by his wife and a handful of friends. Just under a year later he returned, with a Naval escort, to the same spot and an ecstatic crowd of a quarter of a million well-wishers, a full civic reception, and a telegram from Her Majesty the Queen. For the man was Alec Rose, his yacht was the *Lively Lady*, and he had sailed round the world; without fuss, without publicity, and without sponsors, just to please himself. Although this modest gentleman set off with a minimum of glory, he returned to a hero's welcome, and within a week he was knighted at a private ceremony at Buckingham Palace.

Sir Alec was born at Canterbury, and completed his apprenticeship in engineering in the years after the First World War. He emigrated to Canada in 1926 and spent three years there, but they were the years of the great depression, and when hard times culminated in him receiving no wages for his work on an Alberta farm, he judged it time to go back to the Old Country. He liked farming, and bought a small-holding in his home county, working it for ten years; then another war threatened, and the man who had always hankered after the sea, joined the R.N.V.R., to work in the engine-rooms of ships taking part in the dreary convoys of the Northern Approaches. The war over, he left the service as a Lieutenant (E), but the dark days had taken their toll, and a doctor advised sun and fresh air.

The young sailor was an avid reader of sea-stories; he dreamed of adventures in the southern oceans, and an off-duty spell of sailing with whalers had whetted his appetite. In 1951, he started, single-handed, to build his own yacht, a 28-foot ketch. It took him five years, and he called it *Neptune's Daughter*. He remembers it with pleasure and with pride. "A pretty little boat it was," he says with a reminiscent smile, "when I sailed it into the Cornish harbours, the old seamen used to tell me 'you've got a nice little craft there, sir'."

But the oceans were beckoning. Sir Alec had a mind to enter the Single-handed Trans-Atlantic Race, and *Neptune's Daughter* had to go, "though not without a tear", sighs her craftsman. His search for a suitable boat took him to Yarmouth on the Isle of Wight, where he found the *Lively Lady*, a 36-foot cutter-rigged yacht, built in Calcutta of heavy teak timbers. There were fifteen entrants for the 1964 race, including such experienced yachtsmen as Francis Chichester, the Frenchman Eric Tabarley, and Colonel Haslar, one of the 'cockleshell heroes'.

In that, his first race, from Plymouth to Newport, Rhode Island, Sir Alec came fourth, with which he was very well pleased, as he was beaten only by Eric Tabarley, Francis Chichester, and the Welshman, Val Howell. *And* he sailed his *Lively Lady* home again!

By that time, the adventurer had moved to Portsmouth, where he ran a fruit and vegetable shop with his wife. He kept his yacht in Portsmouth Harbour, and thought more and more about his ambition to sail single-handed round the world. In the end it was a casual enough decision; he was fifty-seven, and not getting any younger. With the practical support of his wife, who spent many months listing, packing and labelling stores for the epic voyage (and running the shop while he was away), Sir Alec checked, renewed and repaired *Lively Lady*.

After his simple send-off at Southsea, Sir Alec did not touch land again until he reached Melbourne, where he spent three weeks with the son – also a master mariner – whom he had not seen for seven years, and the daughter-in-law and two grandsons he had never seen. And after that, the long sail home, across the oceans of his dreams.

Sir Alec has written his exciting story in his own book, *My Lively Lady*, but when he is talking of his adventures, he remembers best that great challenge of all sailors, Cape Horn. Then his blue eyes see not the walls of his comfortable cottage in Havant, with his portrait and his trophies, but the emptiness of the South Pacific, the vastness, and the greyness, and the immense seas – what he calls "the great hills of water"; he remembers the snow, the stinging sleet, and the mist; and the cold – the frost glistening on deck and rigging. He sees again the ten-foot wing-span of the fantastic albatross wheeling round his masts, and the grace and tremendous power of the great whales, bigger sometimes than his own craft; he remembers being quite alone, just another of God's creatures, and as such, not lonely.

And God himself was near. Sir Alec has felt a second hand on his tiller when he needed it, and has known a warmth, a glow of comfort in his cabin when times were hard, and prayers had been said. He recalls the sky-reaching columns of spray hitting the huge and incredible rocks of the Cape, and the breath-taking grandeur of the snow-capped mountains beyond. Only for a little while, before the mist descended again; but he saw them.

The voyage took just under a year. There were good moments, and there were bad. But when Alec Rose knelt before his Queen, and felt the sword of knighthood on his shoulder, he knew it had all been worth while.

Ironically, he has little time for sailing now. The *Lively Lady* has been given to a Maritime Trust, for use in training cadets at Salcombe in Devon. Hampshire has no need for a sea-going lifeboat, but his charitable efforts have provided a boat for the Goodwin Sands area at Walmer in Kent, only a part of the valuable work that this resourceful and independent man does for the R.N.L.I. and for young people with a need for that rare quality, leadership.

Not all Southsea's sailing associations are so felicitous, for it was off this shore that the *Mary Rose* foundered and sank on the 19th July 1545, with the loss of some 700 lives. The four-masted, 600-ton carrack was the pride of Henry VIII's navy, and it is said that he watched the disaster from the walls of his castle, listening helplessly to the cries of the drowning men. The *Mary Rose* was built in 1509 on Henry's orders; it carried a full company not only of sailors, but soldiers, pilots, trumpeters, servants, archers, pikemen and gunners, and is thought to have been the first English warship to carry complete batteries of heavy guns on the main deck. It was these batteries that led to the tragedy, for through lax discipline and poor supervision, the lower gun ports were left open, and the deck, barely above the water-line, was swamped, turning the high old ship over.

During the last few years, divers have recovered several of the sunken relics which are in remarkably good condition considering they have lain on the Solent bed for more than four hundred years. There are hopes that it may be possible for the whole ship to be raised, which would cause excitement indeed!

Henry VIII had Southsea Castle built "of his Majesty's own device" in 1544, on the southernmost tip of Portsea Island; having quarrelled with the Pope over his divorce from the unhappy Catherine, he thought it prudent to safeguard his south coast against an expected invasion from France and Spain, and the castle formed one of a line of such defences. The fortress of Southsea was cunningly designed and sited, allowing uninterrupted visibility of the entire seaway. The building is a piece of history in itself, with four hundred years of military interest behind it; inside the warren of vaulted rooms and passages is contained a record of the Portsmouth area, from the flint axe-heads of Palaeolithic man, through ornaments of bronze and cooking pots of iron, to Roman and Anglo-Saxon wares. There are relics too, from H.M.S. *Bounty*, whose crew cast their commander, Captain Bligh, adrift with the eighteen officers and men who remained loyal to him, near Tahiti in 1789; and an exhibition of the block-making machines that revolutionised the dockyard when they were installed there in 1803, designed by the French engineer, Marc Brunel. His son, Isambard Kingdom Brunel, was born in Portsmouth in 1806. He continued the family skills in this country, best known perhaps for his design for the Clifton Suspension Bridge, and the first steamship to be driven by a screw propeller, the *Great Britain*.

Portsmouth has a number of superb museums, with contents ranging from exquisite works of art and beauty in glass, porcelain and furniture at the City Museum and Art Gallery, an imaginative and detailed Natural History display at the Cumberland, and spectacular exhibitions of the history of the Royal Marines who have a long and glorious association with Eastney. For those who, like Rupert Brooke, wonder at the "keen, unpassioned beauty of a great machine", there is the Beam Engine House, a Victorian Pumping Station with a pair of Boulton and Watt beam engines.

One piece of history lost to the city for ever is the house wherein the enduring Sherlock Holmes was born. At 1 Bush Villas in Elm Grove, Sir Arthur Conan Doyle lived and worked at his medical practice, and there he wrote his first novel in which that famous detective appears, *A Study in Scarlet*. Sadly, the house was demolished by bombs during the last war.

Old and new buildings face other with dramatic effect across the Guildhall Square, the city's civic hub; two very different architectural styles; on one side, the new Civic Offices, a tall block with gleaming walls of smoked glass; on the other, the splendour of the Guildhall, rebuilt on its original classical lines after having been reduced to little more than a pile of rubble during the onslaught of January 1941. A local chronicler, W. G. Easthope, recorded that "three hundred raiders dropped 25,000 incendiaries beside high explosive bombs, and at one time twenty-eight major fires were burning with no effective water supply to check them". Those terrifying times must be difficult to imagine for generations who knew them not.

There has been much rebuilding in Portsmouth, with great

new blocks on the sky-line belonging to building societies and insurance companies; also the immense, curved News Centre. Industry and commerce too, are on the increase, with a tremendous expansion of harbour activity. A well-planned continental ferry port was opened in 1976, and is growing fast; it faces Whale Island, where the Royal Yacht *Britannia* lies ready at anchor. Car-ferries and a hovercraft ply between the harbour and the Isle of Wight, and the port handles an increasing volume of cargo, particularly timber, fruit and vegetables.

A major engineering achievement which literally made more of Portsmouth, was the reclamation of land from the sea in the north of the harbour. I.B.M.'s headquarters are built entirely on 125 acres of this new-made land, which also supports a stretch of the M27, a boon to motorist and city alike.

Beyond the flat shore, the stark white chalk rises steeply to form the high ridge of Portsdown Hill, topped by the familiar row of brick forts.

Although the horrors of Waterloo were but a memory in the minds of older folk, the Government was still occupied with fears of a French invasion, to be led this time by Napoleon III, that emperor who fled, ironically, to England after Sedan, to die here in peace. Portsmouth was considered to be a prime target for attack, and following a recommendation by a Royal Commission investigating our coastal defences, the Prime Minister, Lord Palmerston, ordered the building of a ring of forts along the high ridge to protect the town from an attack from the rear, from the landward side, in conjunction with a circle of sea-standing fortresses – the Martello towers still standing in Spithead. The forts were never used, and the whole defence plan became known as Palmerston's Folly, which may be unjust; such malicious tags are easy to establish, but who knows how far the very knowledge of their existence went to deter any invader with designs on our coast?

The sad truth was that war technology was developing rapidly, and politics in Europe were ever-changing, so the forts were obsolete before they were even completed. Their planning was meticulous in attention to strategic detail, and would undoubtedly have been successful if their strength had ever been tried. Built below the crest of the hill, the ramparts were not visible from the north, and an enemy would have come upon them unawares. The forts are a self-contained warren of tunnels, spiral-staircases and gun-rooms, with troop accommodation. The long, sloping tunnels, deep underground, are cut through the chalk, making them chill and eerie. Guided tours are made around Fort Widley, so the tunnels are dimly lit, and a faint green smudge on the white chalk shows where a tiny growth is made possible by the slight warmth of the electric light.

From the ramparts can be seen one of the most spectacular views in all Hampshire – the whole city of Portsmouth spread flat below, with the Isle of Wight beyond, the Witterings of Sussex to the east, and the flames of Fawley's chimneys in the west; wonderful on a clear day, and a veritable fairy-tale on a starry night.

It's a funny place, Pompey. It has an atmosphere all its own, quite unlike any other part of Hampshire, independent, insular, with a permanent sense of bustle and purpose. You either like it, or you don't, there are no half measures. One thing I have always found – the natives are friendly.

V

THE EASTERN COASTLINE

To me, there is something very soul-stirring about Portchester Castle, particularly in the hazy early morning, with the romantic grey walls standing against a background of trees and blue sky, across a stretch of tranquil water dotted with sailing craft, a scene that could belong to any age.

The castle stands grandly on a flat promontory jutting into the north of Portsmouth Harbour, and, approached from the sea, it does not take a lot of imagination to go back fifteen hundred years and see the shore-line of Portchester as mariners saw it in the 400s. The Roman fortress is a much-repaired ruin now, but it must still surely be the most complete example in northern Europe, and ample of the original structure remains to give a fair view of how it looked when primitive vessels of Saxon, Viking and Norman design tied up alongside the sea-wall.

The fort was built at the end of the third century, and the outer walls are practically intact. Just under 600 feet in length and breadth, they form an almost perfect square, with rounded bastions at regular intervals and at the corners; there were twenty when the Romans lived there, but only fourteen remain, the others having been pulled down during later alterations or lost to the sea that laps the eastern wall. Much repair was undertaken during Norman occupation, at which time the fort was already nearly a thousand years old; and now nearly another thousand have passed!

The fort has been more or less in constant used during its long and varied life – as Royal accommodation, for the detention of prisoners of war, for the mustering of troops before a battle, or as a hospital for casualties resulting from such hostilities; and when not in official occupation, squatters and wayfarers made good use of the sheltering walls.

The Roman commander Carausius knew Portchester, as

did his successor, Allectus, and the later Theodosius, in about 370. In 904, Edward the Elder recognised its strategic importance, and two hundred years later, Henry I made extensive alterations.

Many of England's kings spent time there; in 1338 it was made ready for use in the Hundred Years War, and Edward III made plans at Portchester, assembling the warriors who were to fight at Crécy. Henry V gathered his troops, bound for Agincourt, Henry VIII 'made merry' with Anne Boleyn, and Elizabeth visited in 1601, two years before she died. Soldiers were quartered within the walls during the Civil War, and prisoners of the Napoleonic Wars spent long years there. Only last century, a suggestion was made that a hospital should be set up at the castle for the wounded from the Crimea, but the scheme was rejected, and the site of Netley, farther west, was chosen instead. Portchester Castle is in the care of the Department of the Environment now, and enjoys well-justified peace in its old age.

Two of the most notable additions to the Roman fort were made in the twelfth century; the great square keep in the north-western corner, and the church in the south-east, beside the picturesque water-gate.

Henry I founded the church around 1133, as a priory for Augustinian canons, but the monks moved on to another more suitable site soon afterwards, and their domestic buildings were lost. The strongly built church remains, and a register of vicars serving the parish since 1286 is available. The elaborately sculpted arch over the west door is a fine introduction to the Norman treasures to be found within – the font, sturdy, round and much carved, old floor tiles in the chancel, and traces of medieval wall painting above the vestry; there are two 'Sepulchre slabs' of the Crusader period, and much older still, a stone coffin that may have held a Roman child. A coat of arms of Queen Anne informs the visitor that the church was 'Repaired and Beautified in 1710'. Queen Victoria is remembered as well, for at the beginning of the rose-lined path, fragrant in June, is a lych-gate built to commemorate her Diamond Jubilee in 1897.

Considerable excavation has taken place at Portchester, and much detailed information is available to the interested scholar.

Away to the west winds a long creek, the haunt of cormorants. Half a dozen at a glance wing low over the water like lost spirits, or sit on posts, sometimes upright, sometimes with their long wings outstretched to dry after diving for their meal. A lone curlew sweeps overhead, and in winter, whole flocks feed at the water's edge.

At the end of the creek, the mouth of the little Wallington River, stands Fareham, busy now, but busier still when it served as a port exchanging Hampshire grain for French wine. Henry Cort was a familiar name in Fareham at the end of the eighteenth century, when he used coal for experiments in the manufacture of wrought-iron, but ruin faced him when his partner became involved in a financial scandal. The making of 'Fareham Reds', rosy bricks using local clay, was an important industry only recently ended, and the attractive bricks were used to face many famous buildings, including the Royal Albert Hall. Fareham's old West Street boasted a craft recognised by royal patronage, for George III and his successors had their coaches made there until the coming of the railway ended the elegant trade.

A little to the north of Fareham, just outside the village of Boarhunt, or as the local inhabitants will tell you, 'Borrunt', is a well-preserved Saxon church, with a single bell hanging over the east end under its own arch. Typical of the Saxon workmanship is the tall arch of the chancel, only seven feet wide, and the pilaster strip on the east end. Of Saxon date too, is the little window decorated with cable moulding, and also the great font, although this has been much restored. Outside is a huge old yew with a hollow trunk, in which, so the villagers will tell you, a family was housed during a hard winter of long ago.

The water at the mouth of Fareham Creek is littered with moored training ships, some in regular use and others derelict and busy vessels of all kinds chugging about their daily business. Gosport lies on the western shore of the harbour, with a number of old wharves that have seen naval fashions come and go. The Navy's supply and victualling stores have been serving ships since 1753 at Royal Clarence Yard; it stands in Weevil Lane, named, say the uncharitable, because of the uninvited inhabitants of the bakeries where the hard ships-biscuits were made in former years, but this is firmly denied by those whose reputations are at stake, who bring forth evidence of an earlier name for the building – 'Weovil's Storehouses'.

Nearly as old as the Royal Clarence is the yard of Camper & Nicholson, established in 1782. Their yacht-marina is a fine sight, and a fine sound too, as the wind tinkles hundreds of stay-wires against the tall aluminium masts of today's craft. The yard has earned itself a world-wide reputation for first class and 'J' class yachts, including entrants for the *America's* Cup Race, and Sir Francis Chichester's *Gispy Moth II*.

The ferry, saving many miles of road travel, plies across the narrow harbour neck to Portsmouth, just north of Haslar Creek. This inlet eats deep inland as far as Alverstoke, a pretty enough village in past years I imagine, but its Georgian street and attractive cottages are enclosed now by the buildings of a modern suburb.

The focal point of Alverstoke is the church of St Mary, looking like a miniature cathedral, with its square, pinnacled tower and steeply sloping roof. Inside, the feeling is of height and space, and most important, of care and welcome. It is always clean and polished, with gleaming brasses and fresh flowers. Slender clusters of pillars and elegant arches support the lofty centre aisle, and the chancel is gained through a high pointed arch. Stained glass pictures decorate all the windows, and the brass lectern has a round base and lion's claw feet. This, like many tributes in the church, remembers a fallen serviceman, not only in the wars of people's memory, but as long ago as Crimea; for this is essentially a Service Church, and there is a tasteful memorial to those who died in the Second World War on the north wall.

Henri de Blois founded the church, and there is a list in the south porch of its rectors since 1290. It was largely rebuilt in the last hundred years however, a necessity partly due to an enlargement in parish and population in the middle of the nineteenth century, and partly due to the energy and industry of the rector in 1849, Samuel Wilberforce, son of William Wilberforce, who remained for five busy years, until his talents resulted in attaining the position of Bishop of Oxford. He returned to Hampshire in 1869 as Bishop of Winchester.

Along the southern shore of Haslar Creek are moored sinister-looking black submarines. H.M.S. *Dolphin* has been the shore training establishment for the Navy's sub-mariners for more than seventy years. It was at the square diving tower there, 100 feet deep, that H.R.H. Prince Charles made his 'escape' using methods perfected for divers in trouble. The fort on the point of the peninsula opposite the Round Tower of Portsmouth, was built by Henry VI in 1431, to defend the harbour's narrow entrance.

The successful combination of old architecture and modern technology is a happy feature of the Royal Naval Hospital at Haslar; the Georgian brick building is a product of the middle 1700s, but there is nothing old-fashioned about the equipment or the efficiency within. Varied are the uniforms that have passed through the wide gates, for the sick and wounded from the numerous wars since Trafalgar have been brought to Haslar. Many too, are the servicemen who have gazed out of the tall windows, across the banks of gorse to watch the conglomeration of shipping, from the H.M.S. *Victory*, returning with the body of the Commander-in-Chief aboard, to the aircraft carrier *Ark Royal*, from fishing trawlers to hovercraft, all passing the fort at Gilkicker Point, a signal station now, for the currents there can be tricky for inexperienced yachtsmen.

From the stony beach of Stokes Bay, the church spires of Ryde spike the Isle of Wight skyline across the narrow Spithead. The bay is a favourite spot for locals to draw the sea air into their lungs, and for commercial travellers to park their cars on the concrete hard behind the shingle and eat their sandwiches. It is a bleak spot in winter, but beach huts line the road, so no doubt it is a cheerful enough place on a sunny day. I do not feel that I can do full justice to Gosport and its environs, for my visits seem always to have taken place at a cold winter's dawn, or with a drizzly sou'wester sweeping up the Solent. However, Henri de Blois was thankful enough to see the shore there, when in 1140, he found himself in difficulties during a severe storm. Safely gaining the land, he proclaimed it to be "God's Port", and thus the town was named.

The land approach to Gosport, off the A27, is much like the island of Hayling, with narrow, curving roads edged first with market-garden fields, and later by houses and shops. The whole peninsula seems to have been taken over by the Admiralty, with signs to the shore bases of this and that, sprout-

ing everywhere. Any corner the Admiralty missed has been
swept up by the Ministry of Defence, and enclosed with much
mystery.

H.M.S. *Sultan* is the Royal Navy Marine Engineering
School, with laboratories and workshops dealing with ships'
machinery, be it diesel, steam, gas turbine or nuclear power,
and the operation and maintenance of the complicated gear.
H.M.S. *Collingwood*, built at the beginning of the Second
World War, is now, at 196 acres, the Navy's biggest single
establishment, teaching the theory and application of weapons
and electrical engineering. The most popular station with the
sailors must surely be H.M.S. *Centurion*, which deals with pay,
along with accounts and records, but probably the best known
outside the service, is H.M.S. *Daedalus*, the Royal Navy Air
Station, whose helicopters are frequently in the news, having
been called upon for search and air-sea rescue missions, when
yachtsmen or cliff-climbers are in trouble. They have a new
unit too, concerned with giant hovercraft, and the road is
sometimes closed along the coast at Lee-on-Solent, to allow
these cumbersome vessels to cross to the slipway.

In June 1977 more than a hundred and fifty warships
gathered between Portsmouth and Hillhead for the Fleet
Review at Spithead; grey ships they were, grey waters and
grey skies, but a smiling Queen, cheerful as always during the
many public hours of her Silver Jubilee year. Her ancestor,
George III held the first formal Spithead review when he
inspected his naval forces in 1773, and the maritime spectacle
has attracted many sightseers since then.

The windswept acres behind the waves, incorporate the
Browndown Firing Range, and a square-marker on Admiralty charts warns that 'anchoring is prohibited'; hazardous
waters these, it seems, for I am told that a hovercraft pilot was
shot in the shoulder by a wayward bullet a year or two ago,
and that several fishing boats have been peppered!

More than a hundred boats fish the Solent full-time, and
many more take to the sea for casual income or pleasure, for
these southern waters are a plentiful fishing-ground. Quantities are declining though, through over-use according to the
older fishermen. Some of the vessels have a full crew, like the
twin-beam trawlers based at Portsmouth that go out for
several days at a time, fishing the deep waters off-shore, ships

of fifty tons and more; but mostly the fleet consists of smaller craft with self-employed skipper-owners. These warm seas encourage a wide variety of marine life, including porpoises and seals from time to time, and the fishing industry of the area bounded by Chichester in the east, and Poole, in the west, including the Isle of Wight, provides an income at landing value, in excess of £2½ million.

The combination of suitable water temperature and gravelly sea-bed conditions, have made the Solent and its rivers rich in oysters, a harvest for which the south has been noted at least since Roman settlers feasted here. In the Middle Ages, the Hamble River yielded 20,000 oysters, which were sent each Lent to the monks at Winchester, in exchange for much needed clothing. A number of beds, especially in Langstone Harbour and Southampton Water, are still flourishing. The waters off Hampshire's coast are a major oyster-breeding centre, serving all Europe, whose own beds suffered a disastrous disease from which happily, the Solent has remained clear. More than 50 per cent of our young adult oysters are sold to mature in fisheries on the east coast, and for export to continental countries.

Lobsters, crabs and oysters are the most valuable source of fishing-income, with sole a close third; most skippers though, are happy enough to go home with a catch of bass, grey mullet, wrasse, whiting, plaice, skate, cockles, mussels or winkles; and from time to time, everyone drops everything to cash in on the vast quantities of cuttle-fish that pour into the Solent during the early summer. Some years they come, some years they do not; they are neither expected nor looked for. But when word gets around that the shoals have been sighted, the fisherman do not waste any time.

Between the cockle beds of the Meon mouth, and the oysters of the Hamble, the shore line is backed by windswept scrub, but behind it lies a flat belt of fertile horticultural land, with market-gardeners and nurserymen managing fields of greens and rootcrops, and acres of greenhouses.

The sparkling Meon River trickles through marshland to join the sea west of Hillhead. The third Earl of Southampton had the idea of reclaiming the estuary of the Meon, and in 1611 he built a wall across its mouth, which, whatever the worth of his scheme, effectively put an end to the port facilities of Titchfield, the little town on its west bank. To-day's folk know Titchfield for its carnival and Bonfire Night, one of the best organised parades in the county's autumn calendar, but tradition has it that it is the old earl's effigy that is burned each year on the great bonfire, the townspeople's revenge for the demise of their income.

Probably the last establishment of White Canons founded their abbey at Titchfield in 1232, and it flourished over three hundred years into a large community; the monks were much given to reading, and accumulated a fine library of rare books. Margaret of Anjou came to Titchfield as a bride in 1445, to be married to Henry VI; a bridge is there in her memory, known as the Anjou Bridge.

Henry VIII wrecked the peace of Titchfield Abbey. The lovely old building went the way of all monasteries, and the abbey and domestic buildings were given to his Lord Chancellor, who had been instrumental in securing the king's divorce from Catherine. The ruthless Thomas Wriothesley, Earl of Southampton, was thus able to add the glories of Titchfield to those of Hyde and Beaulieu, already in his possession. He set about adapting the interior to suit his comfort, and built a grand turretted gatehouse with four towers on to the nave of the abbey, making a magnificently imposing entrance and hall. The work was completed in 1542, and he called his new mansion Place House.

The second Earl left a large sum of money in his will for the building of a family memorial in the parish church of St Peter, and a very fine monument it is. The church has other claims to fame though, with the remains of a church of great antiquity, possibly as old as seventh century, to be found in the walls of the present tower.

Towards the end of the sixteenth century, a new poet and playwright called William Shakespeare was making a name for himself in London. The third Earl of Southampton became a patron of this promising young man. Some have it that Shakespeare stayed at Place House on several occasions, and it seems likely, but there does not seem to be any conclusive evidence of this. Almost certainly he visited Titchfield though, and it is probable too, that he found material there for some of his works. *Romeo and Juliet* is said to have been inspired by a local love affair, and the name of 'Gobbo' appears in his

Merchant of Venice. Over the years, Venetian vessels called regularly at the harbour of Titchfield, and the name of Gobbo was a familiar one in the area. One such was buried in Titchfield church in 1593, only three years before *Merchant of Venice* appeared on the stage.

In November 1647 the ill-starred Charles I escaped from custody at Hampton Court, and with three loyal officers, rode through the stormy night and all next day, losing his way at times, to the sanctuary of Place House, where he was welcomed and sheltered. But one of his companions put his trust in the wrong man. He brought Colonel Hammond to the house, hoping that he would help the king to find a safe place; Charles knew the man better, and surrendered himself to the unsympathetic colonel; he was arrested, and his fate was sealed.

Titchfield Abbey is a ruin now, with little left of its fateful life but the impressive gatehouse and part of the nave, some fourteenth-century tiles, and walls of a century earlier.

For some reason not satisfactorily explained, these acres of Titchfield, Swanwick, Sarisbury, Park Gate and Locks Heath have proved ideal for strawberry-growing. A combination of soil, which oddly is of relatively poor quality, and favourable early-summer weather conditions have made this probably the most famous strawberry-growing area in the British Isles, providing the season's earliest home-grown fruit. As the railways of north Hampshire took watercress to the country's markets, so, when the Swanwick railway station was opened in 1888, special trains left loaded with punnets of sweet-smelling, succulent strawberries. School holidays were flexible, for picking time was more important than fixed school-hours, and casual labour arrived from all quarters for valuable pocket-money – maybe the same folk who moved on to Alton for the hop-harvest later in the year.

The introduction of polythene has made a great difference to market-gardeners, and has proved a tremendous boon in the strawberry industry. Shimmering tunnels snake over acres of ground, looking, on a moonlit night, like a vast rippling lake. Being entirely undercover brings its own disadvantages however, with pollination a major problem. In 1978, this was tackled by an experiment of breeding blow-flies for distribution within the long cloches – insects easily handled, and efficient, So far, the growers seem well-satisfied with their results.

At the head of the Hamble River's tidal reaches, the small rural town of Botley has settled beside the busy A334. Hampshire's only independent flour mill has been grinding away at Botley for over a thousand years; some say there was a mill there when the Romans were here, a little higher up-river. Certainly "two mills worth 20s" were recorded in the Domesday Book.

At that time, a water-wheel dipping into the river that flows beneath the old building turned the heavy millstones, but in the twentieth century, the equipment is modern, and all-electric. Well, nearly all. Since more and more customers are veering away from 'cotton-wool bakery' and asking for old-fashioned stone-ground flour, the millstones of last century have been put to use again, and they are started into life gently, by water-power.

The mills themselves are an intriguing hotch-potch of styles; the centre building dates from the 1500s, with an incredible tangle of old beams and uneven floors; a pillar in another part shows the water-line of an eighteenth-century flood, with the date marked there by an interested employee. A third side was gutted in a spectacular (and expensive) fire in 1976, and has been replaced by a spacious and airy warehouse incorporating a small laboratory.

The mill has always been essentially a family concern, and remained so when the Appleby family took over the premises in 1921. Two-thirds of the trade now deals with animal feed; home-grown wheat and barley are ground, together with vitamins, minerals and protein materials, to be made into meal and pellets for pigs and poultry. Some of the best farms in the county and more in Sussex, Devon and Cotswold country are supplied from Botley.

The other third of the business is devoted to flour-milling, and apart from the stone-ground wholemeal, steel-rollers are used to produce ten grades of flour used by most of the south's independent bakeries, and by housewives who call at the small retail counter. It is good, strong stuff, with both a high quality and quantity of protein incorporated. I have baked with Botley flour, and there is no comparison with the 'cotton wool' variety.

In 1957, the Institute of Journalists set up a stone monument at the roadside opposite the mill, to commemorate that
'Champion of Free Journalism', William Cobbett. Born into a
rural community in 1763, the son of a small farmer at Farnham, Cobbett remained a farmer at heart throughout his
varied and adventurous life. He achieved his ambitions
through sheer hard work and determination, plus the un-
doubted advantages of an egotistical nature, a belligerent
manner and a prolific pen. Taught by a diligent father the
basics of reading and writing, the truculent and voluble social-
ist used his skills to undertake a number of occupations during
his seventy-two years, starting as bird-scarer at his father's
precious seed-beds when little more than a toddler. The list is
formidable – gardener, soldier, writer, preacher, teacher, reformer, journalist, publisher, farmer, landowner, even courtier
and Member of Parliament. Convict can hardly be included as
an occupation, but he was that too, and Newgate Gaol
accounted for two years of his life, after he was found guilty
of 'seditious libel' through his indiscreet pen.

The role of courtier must have ill-suited the rough and
ready radical, but he was an ardent supporter of Queen
Caroline in the scandals that rocked the polite Georgian
world; indeed, from what we know of the free manners of the
Brunswickian queen, perhaps they had much in common after
all.

For much of his life however, his farmer's heart was firmly
fixed at Botley. He bought a house and four acres there in
1804, and remained for twelve years, writing to a friend that
"Botley is the most delightful village in the world. It has
everything in a village, that I love; and none of the things I
hate. It is in a valley. The soil is rich, thick set with woods;
the farms are small, the cottages neat; it has neither work-
house, nor barber, nor attorney, nor justice of the peace. . . .
Two doctors, one parson. No trade, except that carried by two
or three persons, who bring coals from the Southampton
Water, and who send down timber. All the rest are farmers,
farmers' men, millers, millers' men, millwrights, publicans
who sell beer to the farmers' men and the farmers; copse
cutters, tree-strippers, bark-shavers, farmers' wheelwrights,
farmers' blacksmiths, shopkeepers, a schoolmistress, and in
short, nothing but persons belonging to agriculture, to which

indeed the two doctors and the parson belong as much as the rest." Which not only gives us an insight into Cobbett's mind, but into the rural way of life at that time.

It has changed of course, but not all that much. The Market House that he would have known still dominates the main street, its four fat columns projecting on to the pavement, with clock tower and weather vane above; and the timbered cottages of patterned brick must have been old when Cobbett cantered through in his scarlet waistcoat, on his way to the church and endless quarrels with the parson there. The rural atmosphere is even carried out on the shop-door advertisements, which offer "ferrets for sale", and bulldog puppies, and Welsh Arab geldings, and "meadow hay delivered".

The upper waters of the Hamble are murky now, but there are lovely walks beside the winding river, through meadows and steep woods, ideal just for a stroll, or for the naturalist armed with binoculars and notebook. Even before the busy M27 crosses it, the river has widened enough for cruisers and yachts to be moored, before it reaches Bursledon.

This is the Hamble familiar to users of the A27, and through the arches of the old stone bridge, that favourite haunt of yachtsmen, the Jolly Sailor, can be glimpsed through the forest of masts, its name standing out in large letters to catch the nautical eye. At high tide you can step straight out of your boat on to the forecourt of the inn; at least, I did once, but that was years ago, before the shoals of leisure craft spread to every stretch of water, and probably nowadays you would be lucky to get a mooring anywhere near.

Boat-builders, repairers and chandlers line the roadside, together with great show-piece marinas, right up to the Swan, a large hostelry which is a landmark to drivers on that old Portsmouth to Southampton road.

The lane beside the Swan leads to Bursledon's church of St Leonard, a charming thirteenth-century building, with a tiny timbered west tower and porch, added in the 1800s, and a cool interior, dim even on the sunniest day. Bursledon has the dual personality of a river and rural community, though more and more farm-fields are being taken over for new housing developments. At one time, particularly between 1600 and 1800, the village was famed for its shipbuilding, for the narrow, winding creek was a safe harbour in time of strife, .

and a steady supply of sturdy timbers was assured from the thickly wooded slopes edging the water. Fathers handed their businesses on to sons, and at least one wife carried out her husband's commitments at his death. There was Richard Wyatt, and his son William, and Philemon Ewer, who named his son after himself; but perhaps the best known is George Parsons, who is remembered by a large marble plaque on the church's south wall, for he it was who built H.M.S. *Elephant*, a warship with 74 guns launched at his yard on 24th August, 1786; the wooden vessel served as Lord Nelson's flagship at the Battle of Copenhagen.

Daniel Defoe discovered Bursledon on his travels; it was his sort of place, and he spent a great deal of time there, pottering in the yards and following that occupation so happily described by Grahame's 'Rat', as "messing about in boats".

At the mouth of the river, edging Southampton Water, the yachting centres of Hamble and Warsash face each other across the waves. The College of Nautical Studies at Warsash stands in 120 wooded acres on the east bank of the estuary, with its own pier and landing stage. A residential school, Warsash takes students from all over the world through a comprehensive course of seamanship to the grade of Second Mate. Most of the cadets are school-leavers with ambitions to be officers in the Merchant Navy, and here they are taught just about everything from fire-fighting to naval architecture, from operating a breeches-buoy to demonstrating the principles of astronomy. Much emphasis is placed on putting theory into practice, and the school has its own fleet, with a 78-ton auxiliary ketch, the *Halcyon*, the *Somerset*, an instrument training vessel of 108 tons, as well as a number of smaller boats.

The school was established in 1935 as a school of navigation, but thirty years on, the trends in merchant shipping have changed, as in every other field. New skills are required to handle the giant oil tankers coming into service, and also the great container cargo ships; berthing charges have been increased dramatically, necessitating speedier turn-rounds for vessels in port. A rebuilding programme was undertaken at Warsash, and the school was given a new name befitting its enhanced status and wide range of studies.

While the east bank caters for the world's shipping companies, the west bank is taking care of the airlines. For two decades, the College of Air Training at Hamble has been taking young men between the ages of 18 and 24, and turning them into the pilots who fly the planes of British Airways.

During a twenty-one month course, students are fed on a diet of aerodynamics and meteorology, spherical trigonometry and aviation electronics. The school has its own airfield, with small aircraft like the Piper Cherokee, and after 225 flying hours and many examinations, the successful student gains his Commercial Pilot's Licence – and moves on to start learning all over again with a civil airline. However, he will be a Second Officer by then, and that makes all the difference!

The training at Hamble necessarily involves some night-flying, which is a constant source of friction with local residents. Hamble is a fairly rural area, and night-time operations have been known to be abandoned because of cattle straying on the runways.

Despite these important training schemes, Hamble remains best known for the yacht clubs, marinas and private moorings that spatter the river, and for The Bugle, an inn which has stood near the water's edge since the end of the thirteenth century. The front bar area with its worn flag stones is said to be part of the original building. The unprecedented increase in yachting activity has meant big business for The Bugle, and a large extension has been built to cope with the extra custom.

Yet Hamble is far older than the regattas for which it is now famous, and older too than The Bugle. Roman soldiers feasted on the oysters gathered from the river there, and monks from the priory depended on oysters too, to 'trade' with other communities. The boatyards of the fishing village provided seven ships and the men to crew them, for the battle of Crécy, and later for the growing navy of Nelson's time. Some of the cottages to be found behind the sea-front probably housed some of those very craftsmen.

The coastline turns north-west after Hamble, to edge the busy seaway of Southampton Water. About half-way along, at Netley, Cistercian monks from Beaulieu built their abbey in 1239.

Although Henry III took a special interest in the establishment, it never accumulated the wealth normally associated

Portchester Castle

Hamble

Titchfield Abbey

Itchen Bridge, Southampton

Merchant's house and Westgate, Southampton

Southampton Common

Lepe Beach

Beaulieu River

Hatchet Pond, near Beaulieu

Lymington at dawn

Old street in Lymington

Tuckton

Hengistbury Head

New Forest scenes near Brockenhurst

with such religious communities, which must have greatly disappointed Henry VIII and his favourites when it was dissolved in 1560. It passed into the possession of Sir William Paulet, and when it was later sold to Edward Seymour, Earl of Hartford, Elizabeth I visited him there. For some reason Netley Abbey was not even successful as a home; it fell into disrepair at the beginning of the eighteenth century, and a trip to see the ruins became a fashionable outing for Victorian families. Netley is still a graceful ruin, cared for by the Government, and its many walls include a number of elegant arches, and windows topped with delicate tracery.

One of Henry's defensive South-coast castles was sited at Netley, but it has been a private residence, much altered, for a number of years.

For the crews and passengers of ships voyaging to and from Southampton over the last hundred years, Netley has been best known for the landmark of its hospital, the Royal Victoria Military Hospital. The main building was demolished in 1966, and only the chapel stands now, a landmark still with its minaret-top. The hospital was opened in 1863 for casualties from the Crimea. Whether it is fact or speculation I do not know, but it has been said that the plans of two hospitals were mixed up, the English-style drawings going abroad and the oriental design ending up at Netley. It certainly seems likely, for the hospital was wholly out of place on an English shore, and the wards, which were planned to overlook the shipping lanes and wooded skyline beyond, faced inland. Florence Nightingale never approved of Netley Hospital. It cost the hard-pressed tax-payer half a million pounds to build, and was 1424 feet long, incorporating a hundred beds. But it was inconvenient and difficult to administer, and the lady with the lamp was a stickler for smooth administration.

VI

SOUTHAMPTON

Traditionally, the first piece of England on which new arrivals set foot, is Southampton. From early sailors who pulled their primitive craft into the hamlet on the edge of the salt-marshes, to mink-coated film-stars, stepping into the Ocean Terminal from the luxury of the *Queen Mary*, most of the world came to this island via Southampton. "Gateway to England" the town was proclaimed.

The history of any place is decided by its geographical position, and never more so than with Southampton; few towns have been subjected to more ups and downs, due to its vulnerability in time of war, and its strategic importance for trading convenience.

The city neatly caps the head of the wide Southampton Water, estuary of Hampshire's two most famous trout rivers, the Itchen and the Test. The Itchen flows through the fast-growing town, with the Test forming the south and western boundary.

While earlier tribes preferred the rounded hilltops high above the downs for their settlements, the Romans chose the river-side for their camp, siting their township of Clausentum on the east bank of the Itchen where the land jutted out into a sharp bend, a corner known now as Bitterne Manor. From Clausentum the Romans built roads north to their town that we call Winchester, east to Portchester, and west across the river. There they carried on the business of a port, receiving supplies from home, living a full life in centrally-heated houses, with glass in their windows, tiled roofs and paved floors, eating succulent Hamble oysters from red-glazed Samian platters, and drinking pale wine from green-tinted goblets. They stayed for nearly four hundred years, from early in the first century until the turn of the fifth. Almost nothing is left of them *in situ*, but many relics are on display in the town's museums, particularly God's House.

Succeeding immigrants did not venture so far up-river, and sited their communities nearer to its wide mouth. The Saxons did battle there, and established a fishing village on the west bank. According to the *Anglo-Saxon Chronicle*, the kingdom of Wessex was founded in 519. The spread of Christianity followed and less than 120 years later, the first small church at Southampton was built. A beautiful church stands there still, the sixth to be built on the site, the town's mother church of St Mary, whose bells pealing over the water inspired the lovely old song.

The Vikings ravaged the village as they swarmed round all the coasts, and after Alfred's death, with no-one strong enough to repel the barbarians, the little community was over-run. Ethelred, down in history for ever as 'the Unready', left in haste for France from the harbour, and fourteen years afterwards, in 1016, the young Danish warrior that we call Canute, was proclaimed king of England on these shores, a ceremony which marked an end to the long era of violence and destruction that had torn the south asunder.

The names of Hamwic, or Hamwih were used in those days; the title of Hamtun was also heard, but whereas the first two are variations of the same, it is uncertain whether Hamtun is a further variation, or a separate village just round the curve to the west. Certainly when the Normans came, they used the place called Hamtun, and built a sturdy walled town there, using the quay for regular trips across the Channel to their homeland. These are the 'old walls' that tourists come to see today, and probably the old Bargate is the town's most famous and enduring landmark. This battlemented tower in the centre of the shopping centre once guarded the northern entrance to the walled town, the upper storey serving for many years as the Town Hall, with a prison below. Indeed, it continued to be used in similar style until the 1930s, the Magistrates' Court being held above the police station and 'lock-up'. Much of Norman Southampton is still in evidence in old walls and gates, vaults, street names and churches.

St Michael's is the oldest remaining church, and much of the original eleventh-century structure still stands. Another of the four Hampshire fonts from Tournai greets visitors, just inside the west door, and there are many fine features of architecture and historic interest in the lovely old building, which, like so much of Southampton, was badly damaged during the Second World War.

For three hundred years, the 'town' was confined within the walls, with villages straggling outside, and an Augustinian Priory at St Denys, a mile or so up-river. Medieval Southampton grew swiftly as a merchant port, exporting the valuable and sought-after downland wool to customers across the sea; at the end of the twelfth century, the River Itchen was made navigable from Alresford on the downs, right through to the port, so that barges could move the wool-packs with ease and speed and in greater quantities than road travel would have allowed. The great Fair of St Giles at Winchester brought travellers and traders from far afield, which no doubt added much to the town's traffic. Shipbuilders and chandlers were busy, and merchants grew wealthy. Street names – Porters Lane, Butcher Row, Brewhouse Lane, Simnel Street, Market Lane, Orchard Place, are testimony to the varied occupations, and though their faces have changed, the streets are there still. Galleys and carracks from Genoa, Florence and Venice brought spices and wine, glass, silk and gemstones, and took away wool from the downs, and tin from the mines.

While the history of Portsmouth is largely concerned with affairs of war, Southampton has always been associated with trade, though it has had its military occasions too, and has been the major English port of embarkation for troops in hostilities from Crécy to Suez. It has traditionally taken the blame for bringing to the island the dreadful Black Death plague, but a new school of thought has now absolved the town.

In tiny Winkle Street, adjoining God's House, was established King Edward VI School in 1553. £100 had been willed for this purpose by William Capon, a notable churchman, and a contemporary and associate of Henry VIII's advisers, Cranmer and Cromwell, and especially of Thomas Wolsey. Cardinal Wolsey had obtained the sovereign's permission to follow the earlier example of William of Wykeham who had established the two colleges at Winchester and Oxford, and Henry VI who achieved the same success at Eton and Cambridge; Wolsey's interests were to be Ipswich and Oxford. But he fell from royal favour over his refusal to co-operate in the vital matter of Henry's divorce, and it led ultimately to his death.

The college at Ipswich failed, but William Capon had been much involved in the project, and he retained his interest in education. He had associations in Southampton, and on his death, bequeathed a sum for the "erection maynetenance" and fyndinge of a gramer scole there". Formal consent was given by the monarch, King Edward VI, and the little school was duly opened.

After two moves of location, it settled finally in Hill Lane in 1938, and places there are much sought after. It is a proud school, with a fine academic and sporting record, and Old Edwardians are to be found at the top of their chosen professions, particularly in Government, law and the church. The School Governors remained steadfast in their refusal to 'go comprehensive', and after a lengthy legal wrangle, they have had to revert to independent status from the 1st September, 1979.

At the death of Edward VI, his sister, Mary succeeded to the throne, and her bridegroom, Philip of Spain, landed at Southampton's quay the next year, in 1554. Much pomp and ceremony attended his arrival and his journey to Winchester where he was to marry the queen in the cathedral.

Intolerable religious persecution continued to mar the Tudor reigns, and spilled over into the Stuart era, and August 1620 saw the two vessels *Mayflower* and *Speedwell* leave the country, filled with non-conformists wishing to set up their own free community in the New World across the Atlantic. The Pilgrim Fathers they are called now, and a tall column opposite the Royal Pier commemorates the day they sailed away from Southampton. The two ships put into Plymouth for repairs to the *Speedwell,* and the *Mayflower* eventually made the hazardous crossing alone. Brave folk they must have been, setting off in their little craft across the great ocean, to face they knew not what dangers or hardships.

While the children of those pioneers spread the gospel in the area of Cape Cod, another notable non-conformist was supporting the cause at home. He was Isaac Watts, a cloth-trader, and in 1673, two familiar Southampton names were brought together when he married Sarah Taunton. They set up home in a small house in French Street, and a year later, the first of their nine children was born, a boy; he too was named Isaac.

The father was imprisoned and fined on several occasions for non-conformity, but he persevered, and in 1688, an Independent Chapel (there is one there still) was opened in Above Bar, where he served as deacon. All his children were baptised there, and the young Isaac's name is the first one in the register. He attended King Edward VI's School, and did well there. Having a talent for writing verses, he noticed the poorness of the hymns used in church services, and spoke of it to his father; he received the best advice that can be given – try and do better yourself. The young man did so, with great success. Now his hymns are sung in churches the world over. More than six hundred he wrote, with a longer list under his name in most hymn-books than any other, with the exception of Charles Wesley. One of his best-loved verses, "O God, Our Help in Ages Past", set to W. Croft's tune "St. Anne", rings out from the Civic Centre tower every four hours throughout the day. He died in November 1748, and his statue is the centrepiece of a park that bears his name.

Mrs Sarah Watts had a newphew, Richard, and the cousins were good friends. While Issaac made his career in theology, Richard's talents lay in education; his name is perpetuated too, in the school now called Richard Taunton College.

Even until 1700, most of Southampton was still contained within the Norman walls, but the eighteenth century saw much expansion. The town was cramped for space, and the accumulated fortunes of successful merchants were used to build larger houses in the green countryside beyond. The attractions of the waterside were being discovered, and royal patronage brought a hint of fashion; the growth of coach travel meant easier access for travellers. An influx of wealthy visitors called for improved amenities to tempt open their purse-strings. Assembly Rooms were built, with bathing and promenade facilities; a theatre was opened, and a bank, and there were circulating libraries, coffee-houses, and newspapers to read; and of course, hotels to house the guests.

Of the six main coaching-inns, two still flourish, almost side by side in the High Street – the fifteenth-century Dolphin Hotel, rebuilt in 1775 to cope with the increased trade, and well known for its lovely bow-windows, and the Star, whose arch-wall bears the plaque "Coaches for London and Salisbury connecting with those for Bath and West". The Dolphin's main restaurant is called The Thackeray Room, after the playwright who visited there; Jane Austen was a guest too, and so later, was Queen Victoria. The Star housed the Queen as well, when as a girl of twelve she stayed there with her mother, the Duchess of Kent.

The tiny Red Lion remains also, and the timbered Duke of Wellington in Bugle Street, and farther away from the town centre, at Northam, the red-brick Old Farm House bears the date 1611 across its frontage.

Packets sailed to the Isle of Wight daily, and one-masted coasters plied several times a week to Portsmouth; later, services were extended to the Channel Islands, and even to the French coast at Le Havre. With the growth of activity and wealth, came an increase in cargo-handling. The old quay was no longer adequate, and influential ship-owners began building their own wharves along the Itchen's west bank, where ships topped by billowing sails brought timber, coal, iron, grain and building stone.

For the building trade was booming too, with terraces of elegant Georgian houses spreading far into the new suburbs. Augusta Gordon lived in one of these smart grey houses, in Rockstone Place. Miss Gordon lived a quiet life, and worshipped regularly in St Luke's Church, not half a mile away. When her brother stayed with her, he too prayed there, for he was a devout man.

Major-General Charles Gordon of the Royal Engineers, was virtually 'born into the army' in 1833, when his soldier-father was at Woolwich. Though his military service was outstanding, I have sometimes felt that he might have preferred to do something else with his life, other than soldiering. A shy man, compassionate and kind, he seems to have been happier working among the poor; he knew no fear, had an implicit faith in God, and a careless indifference to death. When he left the family house at Gravesend, he had no real home, and stayed often with his sister in Southampton.

After serving with distinction in the Crimea and China, Gordon went to the Sudan, and at Kartoum, just two days before his fifty-third birthday, he was killed. Queen Victoria was greatly distressed, for she thought a great deal of this modest, God-fearing man; she never forgave her Prime Minister, Mr Gladstone, who she blamed for not sending the gallant soldier proper support.

General Gordon is remembered in Queen's Park, opposite the dockland, as a soldier, administrator and philanthropist; his memorial has a stone base and a cross at the top, with clusters of marble columns between. It quotes the ending of his last letter to Augusta: "I am happy, thank God, and like Lawrence, I have tried to do my duty." His sister's house in Rockstone Place is also identified by a small plaque.

In the year of Charles Gordon's birth, the Royal Pier was opened at Southampton. The first steam-vessel the *Prince Coburg*, had chugged away from the quayside thirteen years earlier, and there were regular trips to and around the Isle of Wight, and excursions to Torquay, Brighton, Portsmouth, the Channel Islands and France.

Southampton's shipping trade was so advanced that it was necessary to build better, purpose-designed docks. Although the pier had been opened in 1833, it was not enough, and the foundation stone for Southampton Docks was finally laid in 1838; the first berth was in use four years later, and the town's reputation as England's foremost passenger port was assured. The shipping-lines arrived, their names changing over the years: P & O, Royal Mail, White Star, Union Castle and Cunard. The big ships came too, names that are part of Great Britain's history.

From Southampton, in the spring of 1912, the mighty *Titanic* sailed away to America on the North Atlantic crossing, with more than two thousand people aboard on her glittering maiden voyage. For the 'unsinkable' pride of the White Star Line, it was her first and last trip. While the passengers frolicked the evening away, the great vessel ran into an iceberg, and went down with the loss of fifteen hundred lives.

Despite the stunning tragedy, the port was entering its golden era, home-base of the world's most luxurious ocean liners and a fleet of cargo-ships; the docks were a constant bustle of boat-trains and elegant baggage, travel-agents and hotel-representatives from Claridges, the Savoy, the Dorchester and Grosvenor, resplendent in their various uniforms, stewards, bell-hops, holiday-makers piled high with wicker chairs from Madeira, bunches of chincherinchees from Capetown and long stems of green bananas from the Caribbean; and the most romantic of all, the two magnificent monarchs of the North Atlantic, the *Queen Mary* and the *Queen Elizabeth*. It was a sad time when they left the port forever.

Although progress had made its inevitable mark, it took four years of air bombardment during the Second World War to change the face of Southampton. With its docks and its Spitfire factory, Southampton was the target for fifty-seven raids during the blitz of the early 1940s; the town was devastated by nearly three and half thousand bombs. A vast area was flattened to rubble in one night, a few disastrous hours when old and beautiful churches, shops filled with valuable merchandise, theatres, cinemas, warehouses and factories all crashed to the ground in an inferno of flame that seemed to engulf the whole world. Only the medieval Bargate stood, right in the middle of the charred and smoking desolation.

What of Southampton in the 1970s? Inevitably, its character has changed. The old walls are still there, well preserved, but the city has spread far in all directions. It is a splendid shopping-centre, with all the major names represented in the multiple stores.

It must be one of the greenest cities in the land, with many beautiful parks right in the town-centre, and others in the suburbs. Mayflower Park, at the water's edge, has proved an ideal venue for the Boat Show, which has become an annual and lucrative event in September.

There is a lovely common too, tended certainly, but allowed to grow naturally, with thick woods, lakes and wide open grassland, and in one corner, to residents' initial displeasure, Chipperfield's opened a small zoo.

Beyond the common, an extensive Sports Centre was established in the 1930s on undulating, wooded land, one of the first of its kind, with a golf course, tennis courts, football and cricket pitches and bowling greens, together with cycle and athletic tracks; and for the less energetic, it is a very peaceful place in which to stroll. A 90-metre artificial ski-slope has recently been opened, and in the hope of attracting major international events, an all-weather synthetic-composition surface has been laid on the athletic track.

In addition to these sporting spaces, national and sometimes international cricket matches are played at the County

Ground near to the Common, and The Dell is 'home' to the First Division 'Saints' football team (in 1978), and a temporary home, during 1976-7 of the coveted F.A. Cup.

Southampton is not all sport, and the town's focal point is the Civic Centre, which was built between 1932 and 1939, to replace the long-inadequate facilities of the Bargate. Numerous other councils have copied the idea since the war, but Southampton's civic buildings were the prototype. The far-sighted designer incorporated into one great complex a fine Guildhall, Council Chambers, reception rooms, administration blocks, a library, art gallery, police station and law courts, all topped by a tall, distinctive clock tower. The complex was built on the quadrangle of the open space known as The Marlands, and the interior decoration is as impressive and grand now as it was forty years ago, despite the difference in fashions.

It was a dislike of changing times that led to the foundation of the University of Southampton. Henry Robinson Hartley was born in 1777, and grew up in the unsettling era of the Industrial Revolution. He lived in the High Street, and could not avoid the noise and activity that centred on the dock and railway building. Henry Hartley preferred a gentler, more sedate way of life, the pace of the eighteenth century rather than the mechanical nineteenth.

He was a wealthy man, the beneficiary of various inheritances, who decided to create a haven of culture for the advantage of the intellectual few. He died in 1850, and his will was not specifically worded; as with so many families, there were domestic tangles, and a long lawsuit with its attendant lawyers' fees, ate deeply into his fortune.

Despite all the difficulties, the Hartley Institute was opened with much celebration in October 1862 by Lord Palmerston. Lack of finance had made it necessary to delay two of the more ambitious projects – an observatory and botanical gardens, but there were a lecture-hall, reading-room, a museum and public library; the founder's wishes were somewhat overlooked, and the establishment was not confined to an élite few, but was open to general use.

The college has had its ups and downs, but in 1902 it was granted university status, and new buildings were opened in Highfield in 1914. Later still, the dignified dull brick halls rose each side of University Road.

Since the end of the war, unbelievable changes have taken place, with immense growth in all departments, advances in technology and equipment, huge new skyscraper buildings, and an unprecedented influx of students from all over the world. Henry Hartley could not be other than proud, but it is not quite what he had in mind.

Most of Southampton's museums are contained within old buildings, the Bargate, Tudor House, God's House and the Wool House, which is devoted to maritime matters. The exception in the R. J. Mitchell Museum, a new exhibition that shows designs and projects of the remarkable Reginald Mitchell. He is best remembered as the designer of the Spitfire, the valiant little plane that made so much difference to the outcome of the decisive Battle of Britain; but before the Spitfire, he had won many awards, and had repeated successes which won for Great Britain the Schneider International Air Trophy. In terms of glory, the Spitfire was his greatest triumph, but Reginald Mitchell was a chronically sick man, and he died just before the war of 1939 was declared. We must be thankful for his foresight.

For a town traditionally connected with water traffic, Southampton has had a great deal to do with aircraft large and small. Bert Hinkler lived on the outskirts while working at Hamble as a test pilot, and in February 1928, he set off in a tiny single-engined biplane, bound for his native Australia, the first person to do so in a light plane. The flight took fifteen days. He attempted a second trip five years later, but the plane crashed in Italian mountain country, and he was killed. Southampton remembers him, and a road at Thornhill is named after him.

The city, centrally placed as it is, was chosen by both B.B.C. and I.T.V. as a location for their studios, which opened within months of each other in 1958. Southern Television have premises by the River Itchen at Northam, and near to the docks are sited the B.B.C. South studios, and the local radio station, Radio Solent.

The 1970s have seen major changes in road systems everywhere in Hampshire, and from the windows of the B.B.C. offices is one of the best views of Southampton's new Itchen Bridge, an elegant construction across the Itchen linking the eastern suburb of Woolston with the town centre. For years residents used a pair of floating-bridges, hauled across the river on thick wire hawsers, and for half a century, a road bridge had been talked about. It was finally opened in 1977 having taken three years to build, at a cost in excess of £12 million, which the Council hopes to recoup in the form of tolls. Already the bridge is much-used, and well on the way to paying for itself, with a great volume of traffic going straight into the Eastern Docks, for while air travel has brought about a tremendous decline in port activity, the roll-on-roll-off car ferries are much in demand, and there are regular cross-Channel trips out of Southampton.

Cargo-handling has changed too, and the coastline of west Southampton has been reclaimed and extended to cater for the new Container Terminal, with extra berths stretching right to the town's western boundary. Container ships mean container lorries, and roads to carry them, and Southampton looks to the future.

VII

THE WESTERN COASTLINE

A conglomeration of roads old and new mark the western exit from Southampton, with a spur road to the new M27 at Redbridge, a fly-over to the town for through traffic, and a wide causeway over the River Test built beside the centuries' old pack-bridge, which was the only crossing to the west until 1930.

To the right, the river view is of thick reed beds winding away towards Nursling as far as the eye can see. Straight ahead lies the small township of Totton, much developed in recent years after the rather stagnant post-war days; a smart new shopping-centre has emerged and also a local Government complex. People of all ages are encouraged to join social courses and attend meetings catering for almost every interest.

To the left, the river heads away to merge with Southampton Water, and a succession of tall chimneys jut into the sky above the west bank.

Sandwiched between Totton and the industrial buildings is little Eling, at the end of the Test's lowest tributary, Bartley Water. This small stream, trickling gently in from the depths of the New Forest, starts life around Minstead, and spends much time between mossy banks before widening out suddenly like so many of Hampshire's south coast waterways, to become a small yachting haven. An anachronistic toll-gate guards the bridge at Eling Mill, the only one left in the county as far as I know, now that Hayling's toll has been withdrawn, except for the charge to cross Southampton's new bridge.

It is worth going through to visit the church on the top of the rise, overlooking the water. Indeed, a footpath through the churchyard leads down to the river's edge, a favourite spot for picnics.

John Pinhorne is buried there, an 'old boy' of King Edward VI School in Southampton, who returned there as Headmaster

109

in 1689. Isaac Watts was a pupil of his, and wrote a verse in Latin to his mentor, thanking him for his kindly teaching. He became vicar of Eling, and later of Leckford, and died at Eling in 1714.

There is too, a wry little verse, composed, presumably by mourners, in 1703:

> Stop, reader, pray, and read my fate,
> What caused my life to terminate.
> For theivs by night when in my bed
> Broak up my house and shot me dead.

So much for the 'good old days'. Eling's parish registers started in 1538, but parts of the church are much older than that, and include an arch from Saxon times.

The western shore of Southampton Water has seen many changes since the end of the last war. It is a working coast now, bleak, flat and uninteresting, although the industry is well shielded by wooded landscaping from the landward side. I can remember when the shore was thickly covered with bluebells, but though these are mostly gone now, the new road constructed to cope with Esso traffic is still lined with catkins and pussy willow, and I always seem to see the first green of hawthorn showing in the hedgerows there, before anywhere else.

On the water-side, red marker buoys with painted names like 'Black Jack' and 'Hythe Knock' guide shipping along the deep-water channel; fishing boats are anchored, their lines floating from propped rods, and grey barges ar lined with black-headed gulls that swoop after the ferries – small boats plying from Southampton to Hythe, larger boats to Cowes, and larger still, to France. Passenger liners are few and far between nowadays, but cargo and container ships still come and go, and great oil tankers are moored along Esso's off-shore jetty.

Opposite Southampton's container berths are the twin chimneys of Marchwood Power Station, a landmark since 1955. The 148-acre complex was built entirely on reclaimed marshland, and takes its cooling water direct from the river, pumping it back again at the end of the process. The warmth of the outflowing water has had a beneficial effect on the fishing ground in the out-pipe's vicinity, particularly on the clam-beds; they were established there accidentally, presumably discarded from the kitchens of the transatlantic liners, and now thrive in commercial quantities. But, say the fishermen, the mud farther along, between Hythe and Fawley, is dead, and nothing grows there at all, a sobering thought.

The heavy crude oil used at Marchwood, thick and black like pitch, comes from the Refinery at Fawley, thousands of tons, by tanker and by underground pipeline. Fuel bills account for something like seventy-two per cent of the Station's running costs, and boardroom price-haggling between the two interests is unceasing. The oil, burning fiercely in vast furnaces, heats pure water to a super-heat of 950 degrees Fahrenheit, at 900 lb per square inch, and in due course, the generated electricity is passed through the transformer to the grid system.

One of nearly 170 power stations in the country, some using nuclear energy, some coal and others oil, Marchwood is about half-way through its working life. Towards the end of this century, it will wear out. A new power station is already in use, built between Fawley and Calshot, equipped with all that modern technology can supply. It will take over Marchwood's role as well when it dies, and by then, probably the new Station will be considered old-fashioned!

Indeed, Southampton Water's west bank is one long strip of advanced technology, from Marchwood in the north to Calshot in the south. 1957 saw the beginning of a great new development near Hythe, when the first turf was cut at the site of the International Synthetic Rubber Company. In less than twenty years, I.S.R. became the largest business of its kind in Europe, satisfying the needs of a world demand; in 1970, the firm won the Queen's Award to Industry.

It is a mysterious place, where the talk is of co-polymerisation and carboxylated latices, styrene-butadiene rubber, and pressure agglomeration processing. The world requires nearly eight million tonnes of synthetic rubber a year, three million of which are consumed by the United Kingdom.

The great complex of I.S.R. houses a department of scientific research and development which is vital to the company, and the effects of their findings are far-reaching – even to farming, where a mixture of latex and oil sprayed on to the land after seed-sowing, prevents wind-erosion of the surface, while allowing the young shoots to penetrate. Like the power stations of Marchwood and Fawley, I.S.R. depends much on Esso for its materials.

It was Esso that really changed the face of Southampton Water, Esso Oil Refinery with its incredible futuristic landscape of flame-topped chimneys, silver-coloured storage tanks, pipelines, gantries and derricks, a trifle chilling by day, and by night a fairyland of a million lights. Its skills and achievements are too massive to begin to include in a book of this kind, but Fawley refinery must be one of the most important places in Europe, if not in the world, supplying almost every facet of our twentieth-century needs. A place of miracles, without a doubt.

Fawley – 'Fauley' on old maps, has a church as old as the refinery is new, All Saints, built in the twelfth century. Then it had a simple nave with a chancel, the two side aisles and the tower being added over the years. The old stone and the flagged floor give the church a rather barren feeling despite the obvious care it receives. One of its most precious treasures, is a paten thought to have been presented by William of Wykeham, and still used for Holy Communion at special festivals.

In the south chapel is a model of a longboat, a memento of the upheaval in the lives of the residents of Tristan da Cunha, a small British island deep in the south Atlantic, just about as far from any mainland as it is possible to get. In October 1961 the volcano on the island erupted; so desperate was the danger, that the entire population of the tiny land was taken off, and removed to the safety of the mother country. Their first new home was a camp in Surrey, but the R.A.F. at Calshot had recently left their married quarters, and in January 1962 the islanders set up their own community in conditions as near to those familiar to them as England could provide. Some felt settled here, but most did not, and in the autumn of the same year, a party of men left for their isolated island to see if it was possible for them to return. Within twelve months, the whole community, with a dozen or so exceptions, had returned to their homeland. The Tristans were faithful attenders at Fawley church, and some of those that remained were married there to local folk.

The thick, stubby chimney of the new Fawley Power Station overshadows Calshot now, and a little to the south, the long spit of shingle beach ends with the lonely coastguard station on the very tip, looking like a miniature lighthouse, with a radar scanner at the top, beamed to the Southampton Port Authority. Beside it are the hangars that housed the romantic old flying-boats, and these dual-purpose vessels were once a familiar sight moored in the sea around the point. The great sheds have been turned into an imaginative leisure centre for young people, who make good use of it. The Coastguard Station stands beside the remnants of Henry VIII's old castle, another of his chain along the south coast, no more than a tower and a few walls now, and quite unattractive. A lifeboat lies just off-shore, ready for use at a moment's notice, for Calshot is on the edge of the busy seaway of the Solent, with the Channel beyond, and there are sandbanks to catch the unwary and inexperienced sailor. The Bramble Bank is one such, forming a sizeable island at the year's lowest tides, so that local yachtsmen and life-boatmen play football and cricket matches there.

The bright red-painted lightship anchored off Calshot Spit has been unmanned since 1973, but until then, it held a lonely crew; they had a cheerful enough job in the active summer season, but it was a bleak post when winter gales and lashing rain swept up from the Channel, or rolling blanket fog isolated them from the rest of the world. At Christmas they were cheered by special deliveries of festive spirit, some of it bottled and some in hampers. It had been intended to replace the lightship with a buoy, but pilots bringing the world's greatest liners along the narrow and treacherous deep water channel preferred to keep the 'ship' shape, which gave them a better idea of wind and tide at that crucial point in turning the vast craft under their control. So the Calshot lightship was reprieved, and continues to send out its warning flash, with a fog-horn governed by the Coastguard Station nearby.

Calshot's shingle beach is backed by a line of beach-huts, brightly coloured and cared for, but somehow, in the way of such man-made villas, they still contrive to look tawdry. I sometimes wonder if it would not be better to see a row of natural-looking log-cabins.

Poaching cannot be a recognised hazard of the sea, but the waters off Stanswood Bay, between Calshot and Lepe, have their own 'gamekeepers', who have been successful in catching and bringing to justice those undesirable characters practising the art. For Stanswood Bay is one of the most prolific oyster beds in the Solent, and is owned by a co-operative of fishermen who guard their interests jealously.

The coastline, a deep red-gold ridge of gravelly, sandy soil, is backed by thick woods, and a line of windswept, crooked pines identifies Lepe, a favourite spot for beach barbecue-parties. Once there were mussels in the Lepe waters, but the crop has been spoiled by parasite pea-crabs, tiny molluscs that make their homes within the larger shells. The beach at Lepe, overlooked by a row of old coastguard cottages, is firmly protected against erosion by timber stockades, stretching right round the bend into the Beaulieu River.

This stretch of the Solent is the yachtsman's paradise, dotted always with white sails, but during the various 'races', and especially during Cowes Week, this prestigious playground is filled with billowing, colourful spinnakers in reds and blues, purples, greens and oranges, in stripes, zigzags, squares, even spots, a gay and wonderful sight, but somehow, strangely undignified.

They spill into the Beaulieu River, some of them into this small, winding river that leads to the romantic Palace House of Lord Montagu. The Beaulieu River is almost unique, in that not only the water, but the river bed belongs to Lord Montagu; I believe there is only one other such in the country. It is unusual too because the estuary is one of the few that looks as well at low tide as it does at full, for the banks are high and straight. Nevertheless, the mud exposed at low water supports a variety of waders large and small, lapwings, oyster-catchers, dunlins and curlews, and a colony of Canada Geese nest on the marshland.

Visitors come in droves to the east bank, to see the gardens at Exbury, which have become one of the sights of Hampshire. The 600 acres of woodland, sweeping down to the river, have been developed since 1922 by Lionel de Rothschild, of the banking family; a gardening enthusiast on the grandest of scales, he imported seeds and plants from all over the world, experimenting and cross-fertilising until he had a spectacular garden and arboretum. It is at its breathtaking best in May and June, for Exbury is especially famous for azaleas and rhododendrons, in more colours than I knew were possible, backed by camellias and many varieties of acer. At the height of their glory, the gardens are an incredibly beautiful sight; the flowering season is a long one, but they are at their very best for only a week or two.

Lanes lined with bluebells lead to the open heath and to Beaulieu, which owes its existence to King John, a man not noted for charitable or religious acts. According to tradition, it was the lack of these characteristics that led in 1204 to the founding of the abbey, for after ordering his horsemen to trample a group of monks who had foregathered to speak to him, the king had a dream which greatly frightened the ruthless man.

It would seem that as a direct result of the vision, he promptly gave 10,000 acres of the New Forest to the Cistercian Order, for the building of a church and dwellings, a farm and a port. The location was ideal, for Cistercian monks were enthusiastic farmers and foresters, and there was much work to be done. Stone was imported from Quarr on the Isle of Wight and from Caen across the Channel, and building began inside a freshly dug earthwork.

When the abbey church was completed in 1246, it was dedicated with much pomp; all the important men in the kingdom were present, including John's son, King Henry III, and all the royal family; Pope Innocent III was also there and gave Beaulieu sanctuary rights, making it one of the five principal sanctuaries in the country. Many were glad to take advantage of this benefit; in 1471 the Earl of Warwick was killed in battle, and the Countess fled there to safety. She remained for two years, but Margaret of Anjou, queen of Henry VI is said to have escaped via the river to France, after only a short stay. The royal impostor, Perkin Warbeck, also sought sanctuary at Beaulieu, but he was tempted outside the safe walls, to be arrested and hanged at Tyburn.

The abbey was dissolved in 1537, and sold the year after to Thomas Wriothesley, who also owned Hyde and Titchfield, and much of the demolished stone was used to build castles at Calshot and Hurst. One of the few buildings left undamaged was the monks' refectory, and this is now used as Beaulieu's parish church, which is why it runs north-south instead of the usual east-west; it has a fine stone pulpit built into the wall, from which a brother would have read to his fellows while they ate their meal, and this unusual feature may have served as a model for the similar pulpit at Northington church. One other of the original buildings also remains, a great barn a mile or so away, at St. Leonards.

Thomas Wriothesley was created Earl of Southampton; Henry, the third earl, was the patron of Shakespeare, and for his part in the 'Essex plot' was imprisoned for life by the outraged Queen Elizabeth. However, she predeceased him, and James I released him and restored his honours and lands.

It was another Elizabeth, the widowed daughter of the fourth earl, who brought Beaulieu into the Montagu family, by marrying Ralph, second son of Baron Montagu of Broughton, in 1673.

In the twentieth century, Beaulieu is best known for its Motor Museum, where more than 200 vehicles from 1895 onward are exhibited; cars vintage and veteran, racing and record-breaking, vehicles commercial and military, motorcycles and bicycles, and also on show are the land-speed record cars 'Golden Arrow' and 'Bluebird'. Visitors can glide above them all on a high-level mono-rail.

But beside all the razzamataz, the abbey ruins, the lovely old church, and the peaceful cloisters are still there.

The west bank of the Beaulieu River is thickly wooded, and there is a footpath south from Beaulieu; the trees are home to a thousand and one creatures, and the walk is a bird-watchers delight, with an enormous variety from green woodpeckers to nuthatches and tree-creepers, and even goldcrests, so small, and so very quick, but given away sometimes by the flash of their bright top-knots.

The unexpected hamlet of Bucklers Hard consists only of one broad main street sloping down to the river, lined with brick cottages. It was the first stage in the development of a new port, and the brainchild of an eighteenth century Duke of Montagu (a title no longer used); the Duke owned various properties in the Caribbean sugar-producing islands, and he hoped to bring the cargo-laden ships to his own doorstep for distribution. The idea never came to fruition, but the little haven did thrive as a ship-building yard, for Beaulieu borders the New Forest, with a plentiful supply of good English oak. At the foot of the street, the Master Builder had his house, and from there he kept a watchful eye on the vast piles of timber left outside to weather and season. At Bucklers Hard were built many ships of Nelson's navy, the most famous of which was the *Agamemnon* in 1781, his flagship at Copenhagen, and part of his fleet at Trafalgar.

Failure to deliver commissioned ships on time brought about the collapse of the industry, and instead of growing into a town, Bucklers Hard stood still.

The little known harbour saw glory again during the Second World War, when sections of the Mulberry Harbour which facilitated the Allied landings in Normandy were made there.

Now the tiny village drowses its way through the winter months, and comes alive in the yachting and tourist season when the one street is thronged with visitors who have come by road or by river. The Master Builder's House has been turned into a very pleasant hotel, and at the top of the slope on the other side, a maritime museum has been opened.

Much of the shore-line between the two rivers of Beaulieu and Lymington is thickly wooded, with the estuary at Lymington edged by flat salt-marshes between which the British Rail car-ferries thread their cumbersome way through the deep water channel on their way to Yarmouth, a pleasant trip of twenty minutes or so. The entrance to Lymington is a mass of yachts, rows and rows, so tightly packed together that their decks are almost touching, and the town seems to have been extended into the water; the interests of yachtsmen and conservationists clashed when plans were proposed to enlarge the marina, but the sailing line had to be drawn somewhere, and no further space was allotted to leisure craft.

To visit Lymington from the waterfront is to see it at its most charming, for the town is then reached via the narrow, cobbled Quay Hill and Quay Street, lined with seventeenth-century houses. It is undeniably 'touristy' now, but nicely so, with hanging baskets, antique lamp-brackets, and painted cart-wheels outside the shops selling cream . teas. Standing sentinel at one end of the steep winding street is the 'King's Head', with a painted sign of Charles II, and a figure-head from the prow of a ship. The Old Customs House, built about 1680, has been converted into an Art Gallery, and the shops of fishing-tackle, yachting-gear and drums of new white rope and webbing are called by nautical names – Captain's Cabin, Flounders, and Shipmates, all a little too quaint perhaps, but not unpleasantly so, and the atmosphere is very comradely.

Lymington has seen its share of warfare over the centuries, and its boatyards have supplied many a navy with warships; the fleet bound for the invasion of France in 1345 was built largely here.

One of the newest boat-builders, providing certainly one of the best success stories of the 'local boy made good' type, is the firm of J. C. Rogers. When Jeremy Rogers left school in the mid-1950s, he did not know what to do with his life, and since his great interest lay in sailing dinghies, he became apprenticed to a local ship-building company as a shipwright. His ability proved to be outststanding, and he left his employers to build wooden dinghies himself, at home. His customers were well-pleased, and Jeremy was thrilled to be asked to make a larger boat, of 26 feet. Orders flooded in, and it became necessary for him to find proper business premises; he acquired a shed and a plot of land at the end of Gosport Street, by the water, and, still strictly a one-man-band, started business in earnest.

The turning-point came in the early 1960s, when one of his customers, David Sadler, asked Jeremy to fit a fibre-glass deck to his boat. The boat was raced with great success at Poole Harbour, and the fibre-glass Comtessa was born. The Comtessas crossed the Atlantic, and were entered for the Round Britain Race. David Sadler designed a 32-foot Comtessa, and Jeremy Rogers built it. A fleet of fifty have appeared at Cowes Week, and in 1975 this was the only fibre-glass yacht to be given its own class there.

Three Comtessa 32s were entered for the 1975 One Ton Cup, a major international competition held that year in England at Torbay; they came first, second and sixth, and it was the first time that the Cup had been won by Britain.

In 1977 a bigger yacht was built for the prestigious Admirals' Cup Race; it was launched only four weeks before the start, almost too late to be selected. Opposition was tough, and critics said the boat could not possibly be worthy of the race, as it was built in too much of a hurry, and not given proper trials. The Comtessa 43 won the race.

In 1978, the firm of J. C. Rogers employed nearly two hundred staff, with an annual turnover of £4 million. And now the Royal Ocean Yacht Club have chosen one of their designs to take part in the new-style one-design off-shore races. They are the only sailing-yachts to be built by injection-moulding process to ensure identical shape and weight; they were tried out during Cowes Week, came second twice, and won once, and went straight on to win the 600-mile race to Spain on handicap. Not bad for a local boy who did not know what to do when he left school.

Lymington's main shopping street is long and straight, and a Saturday market is held there each week. The church of St Thomas stands at the top, its cupola top, with belfry and weather-vane a landmark. It has an unusual interior with a gallery, and was much altered in 1910.

The lanes around Lymington are perfumed with honeysuckle which is entwined in the high hedges, making evening strolls in the June dusk a real delight. On the west side, behind Pennington Marshes grow blue scabious, purple marjoram and yellow toadflax, and like Langstone, the marshes are a favourite haunt of over-wintering migrant birds, and of the hardier residents. The coast sweeps round to Keyhaven, which has been called "a strange corner that isn't really anywhere", an apt description. It is a tiny yachting haven between the marshes and Hurst Point, a steep spit of shingle; reminiscent of Chesil Beach, and covered by the sea at high tide. It is a mile or more long, and a hard walk for the energetic, but there is a ferry in service at certain times to take visitors from Keyhaven to Hurst Castle; at the end of the Spit. This is the most westerly of Henry's defensive forts, and ideally placed for guarding the Solent. Whatever his faults, Henry VIII was no fool as a strategist, and his fort was used when invasion threatened right up to the Second World War. Across the narrow channel are the white cliffs of the Isle of Wight, with Fort Albert at the point, and the ragged outcrop of rocks, The Needles, in the distance.

Hurst Castle was built from the stone of Beaulieu Abbey, and completed in 1544. Low and curved at the seaward side, it has a high tower, and the ghostly figure of a monk is said to have been seen there. King Charles was lodged there overnight, under guard, on his way from Carisbrooke to London in 1648. There are two lighthouses on the Point, a tall white tower to mark the tricky 'narrow', and a low red one right on the Point. The old wells are no longer used, and a fresh water supply is taken from Yarmouth every day to the few hardies that live on the spit.

Off-shore, near Milford, a local firm is experimenting with and researching wave-power energy, and three business-like platforms measure the various forces.

The cliffs begin to rise from the flat shore, characteristic of the coastline of west Hampshire, and the beach-huts and caravans of holiday businesses start to mar the views of Milford, Hordle and Barton.

All the inlets along this coast have tales to tell about the smuggling days of old (and probably not so old), and about laden carts that rumbled across forest tracks on moonless nights. Spirits, wine and 'baccy for the parson' have always been popular merchandise, and later the iniquitous tax on tea brought it into the smuggled goods category. One such inlet was the quaintly named Chewton Bunny, the local word for chine, or glen.

Chewton Glen House was first mentioned in documents of 1732, a time of expansion in the building of elegant country houses. Just over a hundred years later, the property was bought by George Marryat, and throughout the 1840s, his sailor-brother, Frederick, was a frequent long-term visitor.

Captain Marryat's naval adventures formed the basis for his many sea-stories, but he was also much attached to the forest land around Chewton. While he was a guest there, he gathered material for his last book the ever-popular *Children of the New Forest*. The old story centres around the mansion of Arnwood, and several houses between Sway and New Milton bear a variation of the name; but on the estate of one of George Marryat's friends was a cottage called 'Arnewood', which must surely be the one that influenced the author.

The appearance of Chewton Glen House altered with its many changes of ownership, and in the 1960s, it became a hotel. It is so still, and during the last ten years it has won an impressive collection of accolades.

The beautiful old mansion, in thirty acres of parkland between the New Forest and the sea, is a member of the coveted Relais de Campagne, and has a Four Red Star rating; at the beginning of 1975, it was officially recognised as one of the leading hotels of the world, and the following year, the Chewton Glen Hotel was awarded the Egon Ronay Gold Plate Hotel of the Year.

The historic interest has not been neglected however, and many of the rooms have names connected with Captain Marryat's novels.

VIII

LOST TO DORSET

When that ardent countryman, Ralph Wightman wrote his *Portrait of Dorset* in 1965, his county boundary lay west of Bournemouth, so that the land eastward lay within Hampshire. When, in 1974, with the signing of a few documents, the border was shifted ten or so miles east to Highcliffe, a triangular portion of the county's most interesting land became Dorset, and should not, therefore, be mentioned here; but there is too much of interest to leave it out altogether, for it includes the estuaries of the Avon and the Stour, which meet and flow into the sea at Christchurch, and the mighty headland of Hengistbury, together with the two long bays that sweep in sandy arcs from Milford to Christchurch Harbour, and round again past Bournemouth to the Old Harry Rocks at Studland, breaking only at the entrance to the immense haven at Poole.

Being unsure of the exact location of the new boundary on the coastline, I enquired at a local Council Office, which side of the border Highcliffe now lay. The obliging clerk consulted his wall-map, and told me with much merriment that 'Highclif' was in Dorset, but 'fe' was in Hampshire; which caused great amusement, but was of little help. The local police, however, said that they did not deal with any incident west of Chewton Glen, which seemed to clinch the matter. Highcliffe has been lost to Hampshire.

This holiday town has always been a popular sea-side resort, but its residential and leisure development has spread a good deal in the last two decades. Set roughly in the centre of Christchurch Bay, the beach is backed by sandy cliffs, which have become very unstable over the years, due to sea erosion; there have been some dramatic falls, and large sums of money have been spent on restoration and safety work.

Highcliffe's imposing-looking castle stands at its western

end, something of a white elephant, and lately the subject of much controversy, Lord Stuart de Rothesay had the place built early last century, but in the French style of a much earlier period; indeed, some of the stonework was brought to Highcliffe from Rouen. Edward VII stayed at the castle, and so did his kinsman, Wilhelm II, the German Kaiser, and both planted trees to commemorate their visits. Gordon Selfridge, of Oxford Street fame, lived there too, and is buried in the local churchyard. The property became a training centre for Roman Catholic priests, but they moved out in 1967, since when the building has remained empty. Inevitably, it has suffered damage by vandals, and twice by fire, leaving it a sad remnant of de Rothesay's predilection for grandeur.

Mudeford, just along the coast was a pretty fishing village once, and is still attractive, with old cottages and an inn, a small quay, boats, and fishing nets spread out to dry. This is a choice fishing ground, where the Avon and Stour join to form a narrow channel known as 'the Run' before they meet the sea. For many years, the local minister has held a sea-borne Blessing of the Waters service at Rogationtide, and at the Harvest Festival, fishing nets take their place among the produce of field and garden. Coarse fishing is a major occupation here, with a good chance in the spring of hooking or netting a fat salmon as it heads up-river; there are sea-trout too, and dace, grayling, perch and tench, roach up to 3lb., chub at 5 lb, and barbel at 14 lb., which, not being an angling enthusiast, I have to accept as being a fair size. Maggots are forbidden, but any number of different baits are used, including - unless my youthful informants are pulling my leg - luncheon meat and cheese paste. For sea-fishing there is a variety too, with flounders, pollack, conger eels, dogfish and bream always plentiful, and in high summer, tope and sometimes small sharks.

Sir Walter Scott stayed at Mudeford in 1807, the guest of a friend there, and he spent some time on his poem *Marmion*; Samuel Coleridge found benefit from the bracing sea air several years afterwards, when he recuperated at the village from a near-breakdown from overwork and strain.

Christchurch Harbour, almost land-locked, is a safe place for sailing, although the shallow channel allows only the smallest draft. From the old bridge at Tuckton, the scene is bright with colourful dinghies and gaudy sails.

Christchurch is one of my favourite places, with its serene harbour, and eleventh-century priory that manages to combine beauty with homeliness in the happiest way, and more picturesque nooks and corners and unexpected views than anywhere else I know. The harbour is almost enclosed by the long spit of land guarded by Hengistbury Head, leaving only a narrow gap between the two land masses; a tiny ferry plies between them.

Without doubt, the first community on this stretch of coast was on the great headland, named, I always understood, after the fifth-century Hengist, but I think that this assumption is now contested. However, an ancient earthwork stood on the summit, and an Iron Age village has been reconstructed on the site. Many relics have been found of past inhabitants, including pottery of the Atrebate culture; much of this can be seen at the Red House Museum in Quay Road, near to the Priory.

My first view of Christchurch Priory was from the railway line to the north, standing against the skyline across meadows of buttercups. I loved the look of the grey old church even then, but in those childhood days it was more of a landmark, a sign that we were approaching Bournemouth, land of the long and glorious summer holidays.

With such an old priory, there is naturally much of interest for the visitor to discover. For me, one of its greatest charms is the legend of the miracle, a well-known story which bears repeating.

The church, so it is said, was never intended for the site it occupies, but was begun on a hill about a mile away. Each day, workmen carried their equipment and material to the building site, but each night, what was left was taken by an unseen agent down the hill again. The mystery was interpreted as Divine Guidance, and the men set to work on the second site, where they were joined by a stranger who took his part in the construction, but was always missing at mealtimes, and on pay days. At the end of a long day's toil, a roof beam was found to be too short by about a foot, and the weary workmen left the problem to be sorted out in the freshness of the next day. But by morning, the beam was in its place in the roof; and the stranger was never seen again. The men discussed the miracle, and decided that the Carpenter of Nazareth had been among them; the old name of Twynham was changed to Christ Church. The beam is still there, not in the same place it is true, but I think it is a lovely story.

The peninsula of Stanpit Marshes pushes its long fingers into the harbour, 150 acres designated since 1967 as a nature reserve. Reeds, sedges and grasses thrive on these old saltings – also spartina and scurvy, and the 'sea' versions of lavender, pink and aster, tall velvety marsh mallow, and a dozen others. It is a bird haven too, with avocets and bearded tits recorded, and even ospreys have been seen, and smaller waders abound in their thousands in the season.

Bournemouth has spread east, north and west since Sir George Gervis planned his shore-side village in 1836. For five hundred years, the sandy waste of heathland had appeared on maps and documents as la Bournemowthe, where the scattered cottagers grazed their animals and cut turf for winter warmth. On an Ordnance Survey map of 1809, it was called Bourne Mouth, after the little River Bourne, formed by two streams trickling from springs on nearby Canford Heath, through Bourne Chine to the sea. These steep, pine-clad chines, the delight of today's holiday-makers, were ideal for hiding smuggled cargo from the excisemen in the eighteenth and nineteenth centuries, and much of the coast was so used. No doubt the patrols of the Dorset Yeomanry, on the lookout for Napoleon's ships, interfered sadly with that age-old pastime, but their commander, Captain Lewis Tregonwell, took advantage of the situation, and taking a fancy to the place, settled there, building one of the first houses of the new town.

Bournemouth developed quickly into a fashionable resort, earning an encomium from Queen Victoria which set the seal on its popularity. John Keble settled in a boarding-house near to the pleasure gardens, after nearly thirty years of serving his parish of Hursley, near Winchester. He went to Bournemouth because of the precarious state of his wife's health, but it was he who died after six months in his new home, in 1866, and his sick wife survived him by only six weeks. Keble is remembered in the south transept of St Peter's Church, but his body was taken to his beloved Hursley for burial.

Ten years later, nine-year old John Galsworthy attended a

preparation school in the new town for five years, and Robert Louis Stevenson spent various periods there, writing *Kidnapped* and *Dr Jekyll and Mr Hyde*. Thomas Hardy, a great borrower of real places in which to set his novels, wrote of the town as 'Sandbourne' in *Tess of the D'Urbervilles*.

The holiday town continues to be one of the most popular on the south coast, its amenities growing with every year, its sandy beaches, cliff-top walks, beautiful chines and lovely parks a joy.

There is so much to be said of this triangle; but we should be talking of Hampshire, and this land, alas, is now Dorset land.

IX

THE SOUTH-WEST

Much of the south-western corner of Hampshire is within the area of the New Forest, or the perambulation, as the legal forest boundary is called. The New Forest is almost a kingdom within a kingdom, with its own terminology, laws which relate to it alone, and a background unique in lore and customs.

There can be few places in Great Britain with so varied a landscape in so small an area – deep, thick woodland, with great oaks and beeches, high, windswept heathland, prickly with gorse and heather, water-logged, squelchy bogs overhung with alders, and sun-dappled glades, waist-high in bracken, laced with clear brown streams, only trickles in a dry spell, but purling over the clay beds in wet seasons.

There is Bartley Water, rising near Minstead, and flowing east through Woodlands and Ashurst to join the Test at Eling; Highland Water and Ober Water, mingling before they reach the sea at Lymington; Dockens Water, heading south-west to team up with the great Avon; and the Beaulieu River, arching round Lyndhurst before crossing the purple heath to its estuary in the Solent; also a dozen other small brooks. To the visitor, these are just 145 square miles of land lumped together under the general heading of The New Forest, but to the foresters, there is a name for every enclosure, each clump of trees, every tiny stream, probably even every path.

The forest was 'created' soon after the conquering William had subdued his new people sufficiently to be able to turn his thoughts to pleasure, rather than to battle. There were few pastimes more popular with the king and his sons than hunting the stag and the boar, and he proclaimed the wild tract a Royal hunting preserve 'for the pleasure of the Chase', and placed it under forest law. These were specific edicts, and they made life for the peasants very difficult; they were forbidden

127

to fence their land, or to put up any hurdle which might impede the free run of the hunt; they were not allowed to cut firewood, or to carry a bow and arrow, or to keep a dog, unless its claws were restricted to make it useless for catching game. Their long-established Commoners' rights were inhibited, and poaching was punished harshly, by heavy fines for the fortunate, and blinding or mutilation for others. All 'venison and vert" were the king's, the deer and the boar, even the trees themselves. Special courts were instituted to enforce the laws. It was an unhappy time for the foresters, and for the forest itself, for the poor soil and the sparse growth it supported suffered severely.

The forest laws were no less unpopular with the gentry, whose rights and pleasures were likewise curtailed. Whether they took matters into their own hands, or whether it was an accident will never be known, but what is certain, is that on an August day in 1100, while out in the forest enjoying a stag-hunt between Stoney Cross and Cadnam, the second King William, known as Rufus, was shot with an arrow, and killed.

Some believe that the incident was a planned assassination, a plot known beforehand to many at home and abroad. Certainly no time was wasted in sorrow after the king's death. His brother Henry, one of the party, rode straight to Winchester to claim the throne and the treasury before the news could be taken to their elder brother, Robert, fighting abroad and already once overlooked in favour of William. One of the squires, Sir Walter Tyrrel, who was 'credited' with firing the fatal arrow, spurred his horse to Poole, and sailed without delay for Normandy, while the other members of the hunting-party seem to have decided that on this occasion, discretion was the better part of valour, and dispersed swiftly along their separate ways.

The king's body lay where it fell, unheeded and untended, until a forest charcoal-burner found it. Great must have been his astonishment, and he put the richly clad corpse on to a cart, and trundled it all the way to Winchester. An accident, or conspiracy and murder? Almost certainly the latter.

A small monument, the Rufus Stone, was erected much later at Stoney Cross in Canterton Glen, marking the alleged location, although the precise spot has always been in doubt; a street in Romsey bears a plaque saying that the royal corpse passed that way, and the Kings Way at Chandler's Ford is also supposed to have formed part of the journey. There is too, an attractive hostelry at Cadnam called the Sir Walter Tyrrel, named after the villain, or the hero of the piece, depending which way you look at it.

Even after the death of William Rufus, the forest laws remained, and other 'lesser royals' met their sudden death at the hunt. There was an easing of the situation after the Magna Carta was signed, but it was not until 1217 that the New Forest had a charter of its own, and a slow process of improvement was achieved.

The whole south-western corner lies in the Hampshire Basin, a broad, shallow hollow filled with gravels, sand and clay, fanning out to the west, north and east to the chalk hills of Dorset, Wiltshire and Hampshire. The New Forest has to be carefully managed, for it is a truly beautiful place, and sadly, the people who come to enjoy its beauty are the very means whereby, if due care is not taken, it will be destroyed.

The medieval kings appointed Lord Wardens to preserve the forest; nowadays it is largely administered by the Forestry Commission, and the chief officers are still called by their ancient title of Deputy Surveyor. Their task is to produce timber, some of which is used for telegraph poles and fencing, and a good deal of softwood and trimmings for the pulpwood factories to turn into cardboard cartons and packets – the days when the Forest supplied the Navy with timber for its warships are long since over! The Deputy Surveyors also have a responsibility to preserve wild life, and to safeguard public amenities, and to these ends, much effort has been directed in recent years to the providing of controlled camping sites, car parks and picnic areas. The Commission has little to do with Commoners' Rights, and disputes are still dealt with by the Verderers' Court, a powerful remnant of ancient Forest Law.

This court is held at Lyndhurst, the forest's natural 'capital', centrally placed within the old boundaries, on a rise of land at the meeting of several important trackways. The town is so named because of its situation, and the lime trees which were once a feature there. 'Lin-hest' was a Domesday village, and already a royal manor in 980. It is the only royal manor in the forest, and various monarchs have lived there, from

Eleanor of Castile in the thirteenth century, who passed her time at the Queen's House while her spouse was away fighting the Welsh, to Prince Frederick, son of George III, in 1850.

Like all forest villages, Lyndhurst is quiet in the winter, and bulges at the seams with visitors and traffic in the holiday season. The New Forest's administrative centre is at the end of the village by the church, the Queen's House (or King's House, depending on the current monarch). The Verderers' Court is held there on alternate months, and is open to the public. It is a splendid, old-fashioned room, panelled, baronial and anachronistic, with beams and benches in good solid timber, and walls hung with antlers. The room itself is nearly always open to public view, and is a peep into a deep and fascinating past.

The church stands on a high point, and its tall spire is a landmark for miles. Brick-built and spacious, there are several features to interest the visitor, but perhaps its chief claim to fame is the grave of Alice Hargreaves, who in her young girlhood, as Alice Liddell, was the first of many youngsters to be used as models for stories and photographs by Charles Dodgson. The writer is better known as Lewis Carroll, and his model as the Alice who found herself in Wonderland. She died in 1934, at the age of 82.

Roads lead in all directions from Lyndhurst; the south-east track leads past Bolton's Bench, one of the forest's best known burial mounds, and across the wild heath. There is always a gathering of forest ponies by the cattle-grid at Bolton's Bench; one of the forest's most endearing features is its animals, cows, ponies, donkeys and pigs all wandering freely; deer too, though they are shy, and not always easy to find. In some places geese forage at the roadside.

A high toll of road-deaths led to the fencing of the main through-roads, but elsewhere the driver must still take care, for the animals will stand in the middle of the lane just round a bend, and as they won't move it is usually up to the motorist to take evasive action.

It can be a little unnerving too, to come across a herd of cattle stationary across a narrow lane. They are oblivious to traffic, chewing the cud, their eyes vague, and no honks, shoos and thumps will move them, except to edge perceptibly to surround you, leaving a little metal island amidst a sea of warm, gently heaving cow-flesh.

The animals are not wild of course, they all belong to the Commoners, and once a year the ponies are rounded up, cowboy fashion, and penned opposite the railway station at Beaulieu Road in the middle of the heath land, for branding and selling. Cattle are mostly taken indoors for calving, but the hardy ponies are left to fend for themselves, and young, unmarked foals are claimed by the owner of the mare with which they are running. There are still some donkeys, but their numbers seem to have dwindled since my forest school-days, when they used to gather round the bus-shelter at Brockenhurst, sure of titbits from someone waiting there. Geese are a fairly unusual sight, but in the pannage season, between 25th September and 22nd November, pigs are turned out to rootle around under the trees for beech mast and acorns, so good for swine, but so bad for the ponies, some of whom die from eating them. This vast stretch of heathland between Lyndhurst and the coast is fairly flat, and the poor, gravelly soil supports several kinds of heather, mainly the bright pink bell-heather, and the paler ling, making a soft mauve haze broken only by small humps of gorse and sheets of bracken, with an odd silver birch or Scots pine breaking the sky-line.

Just out of Lyndhurst on the Lymington road, is Foxlease, a name familiar to Girl Guides the world over. The house was built about 400 years ago for a forest-keeper, and called then, Cox Leyes. Only the hall of that old house remains now, low-ceilinged and square, and one or two of the smaller rooms, but in 1775, a new house in the Georgian style was built around the old one, with three rooms designed by the fashionable Robert Adam.

The house and grounds of Foxlease were given to the Girl Guide Association by an American lady, Mrs. Archbold Saund-erson of Washington, on the occasion of the marriage of H.R.H. the Princess Royal in 1922. It was turned into a training centre, and much used; the rooms, which contain unique furnishings of all kinds, are named after the countries or counties that have 'adopted' them. These far-off places have their own training centres now, but Foxlease was the first to point the way; on display are greetings cards from the Baden-

Powell family, and a picture of their garden in Kenya, painted by the founder.

The two streams of Ober Water and Highland Water have already joined together before they pass under the road by the Balmer Lawn Hotel, set back from the road just before Brockenhurst. A picturesque village this, with the rare advantage these days of having a main-line railway station.

The river winds between Sway and Boldre, with Pilley in the middle, and at the inn there, called the 'Fleur-de-Lys', we are back in *Children of the New Forest* country again. Various rooms here are named after characters in the book, and the Jacob Armitage lounge still has the original fireplace, with a recess for an hour-glass and for salt.

The 'Fleur-de-Lys' is an old, old inn, certainly the oldest in the forest, and probably for many miles around. The landlord, Sidney Hayward, son of the previous landlord, has taken a lively interest in his ancient surroundings, and set about tracing its past. He found that the French-sounding name derived from a symbol on the coat of arms of William de Vernums the landowner at the time of King John; he also discovered that the first recorded landlord was Benjamin Stones, who hosted the inn in 1498. Sidney Hayward has compiled a list of landlords since that time, which hangs in the lobby. Long, low, white-washed and thatched, the 'Fleur-de-Lys', French-sounding or not, is as English an inn as you could find.

Typically English too, is the simple church at Boldre, where William Gilpin served his scattered parish for thirty years, after many years of school-teaching. A busy man, he walked a lot, studying the forest and writing about it, as well as looking after a living which had been sadly neglected by the previous incumbent. What Charles Kingsley had yet to do for Eversley, William Gilpin did for Boldre, leaving the parish better in every way than he found it, and what better epitaph for a man? At Boldre, in 1839, Robert Southey was married to his second wife, Caroline Bowles, a poet in her own right, and a writer in the style of Charlotte Yonge, showing charm and simplicity.

The road south-west from Lyndhurst passes a pretty corner of thatched cottages opposite the long-used cricket-pitch at Swan Green (not to be confused with Goose Green, which is on the way to Brockenhurst!); and heads for Christchurch, with a smaller road branching off to the right for Burley.

This is the deep forest that strangers expect, with dense, tall trees, and quiet plantations of dark, pluming conifers. A tarred pathway wide enough for cars crosses the main road just before the Burley turn-off; it is the Ornamental Drive, with Rhinefield on the left, and on the right, an arboretum of rare and beautiful giants, all labelled for easy identification. There are sequoias, Wellingtonia and Californian redwood, Mexican pine, Columbia red cedar and Sitka spruce from Alaska, a spectacular sight at any season, but especially so in the spring and autumn.

But the most magnificent of them all, is a good old English oak, the Knightwood Oak, said, and who shall doubt it, to be the largest and the oldest oak in all England. Its girth is nearly twenty-four feet, and it has stood in the heart of the forest for at least 400 years. It is an awe-inspiring sight, and worthy of more than a moment's pause, to wonder at this fantastic piece of nature's engineering. But even the Knightwood Oak will not last for ever, and in April 1979, to mark the nine-hundredth anniversary of the New Forest, Her Majesty the Queen planted a sapling nearby, said to have been grown from an acorn of the old veteran

It is beside the winding road to Burley that I have most often seen roe or fallow deer, deep in the woods, a wary stag sometimes, with his small herd. Burley is the heart of 'witch country', and it is said that there is a coven of 'white witches' established there. The forest has never been short of witch stories, and Burley has made the most of them by calling its tourist shops the 'Witches' Coven' and 'Sorcerer's Apprentice', and so on.

Another man deeply interested in the supernatural lies under a large oak in the graveyard at Minstead, a hamlet on the north road out of Lyndhurst. A simple cross marks the grave of that most remarkable man in an age of remarkable men, Sir Arthur Conan Doyle. Though his name is of course familiar, it is strange that his creation should be even better known. So compelling a character is Sherlock Holmes, and so real a personality is Dr Watson, that it is almost difficult to remember that they belong to fiction.

Arthur Conan Doyle was born in Edinburgh in May 1859,

a period of dismal depression for that fine city. He combined a basic goodness and sense of propriety with a mystical romanticism, and an ability for story-telling that stood him in good stead during his bleak schooldays. He returned to Edinburgh to study medicine at the university, and took work later as a ship's surgeon, where he wrote tales during his leisure time, and told stories to his shipmates to beguile tedious hours.

When he left the sea, he set up a general practice in Southsea, waiting in extreme poverty for his first patients. They came at last, and he married a relative of one of them. If patients had been quicker to fill his consulting rooms, perhaps Sherlock Holmes would never have been born, for it was during his idle hours at his Southsea home, that the hero evolved, and there the first Holmes story "A Study in Scarlet" was penned. The manuscript was returned unread; the second publisher accepted it, and bought all rights for £24, and the story appeared in a Christmas annual in 1887. It received excellent reviews, and was sold in book form the following year. Success was to follow, and the author travelled widely at home and abroad. It was during this period that he spent much time walking with a friend in the New Forest, and discovered Minstead; the village appears in his novel *The White Company*. One of his greatest admirers was King Edward VII, and in 1902 Arthur Conan Doyle was invited to Buckingham Palace, where a knighthood was conferred upon him.

His life was not without sadness; his wife's health was failing, and she died in 1906. However, although he had remained faithful and devoted to her, he had for several years loved another woman, and he married her the following autumn. They bought a house in Sussex, and he found time to develop his long-time interest in spiritualism; he wrote mystery plays, and ghost stories. Doyle was a man of many parts and varied skills, much ahead of his time.

It was not until the later 1920s that he made his second home at Bignell Wood, near Minstead, and rediscovered old haunts explored nearly forty years earlier. Bignell House was secluded, a requisite for his increasing obsession with the spirit world; he held seances there, to the displeasure of his neighbours.

In July 1930, he was to find out for himself what lay on the 'other side'. He died at his home in Sussex, aged 71, and was buried there; his widow, who shared his beliefs, was convinced that she received messages from him. After her death, the family moved the two bodies in 1955, to the graveyard at Minstead; they lie together beneath a stone inscribed with a tribute to the way he lived: 'Steel True, Blade Straight', Knight, Patriot, Physician, and Man of Letters.

The church itself is a quaint place, built in pale brick with a west tower, and it has a cottagey look which is caused by the little dormer windows in the steep roof. There are many interesting things to see, perhaps the most unusual feature being the three-tiered pulpit; the first 'deck' was used by the clerk, to say his 'amens', the second for the biblical readings, and the third for delivering the sermon.

One of the most exclusive private pews to be found in any church is here too, a comfortable sitting-room with upholstered seats, a window, even a small fireplace, and it was entered by its own door from outside. It was for the residents of the 'big house' at Castle Malwood, and their eyes would have been on level with those of the preacher, causing discomfiture to both on occasions no doubt.

Minstead is very much a forest village, with a green where ponies are always forgathered, and an inn of character called 'The Trusty Servant', with a famous sign.

Furzey Gardens are here too, a venture which was the idea of Bay Dalrymple, one of three brothers who came to the forest in 1922. His brother Hugh, set up nurseries at Bartley, just a few miles away.

The present owner is Mr H. J. Cole, and the eight acres of gardens are open to the public every day of the year. Springtime is best at Furzey, when bluebells mix with a myriad of other bulbs to make a mass of colour, forming a background for azaleas and rhododendrons, and many other shrubs.

Furzey has an 'ancient cottage', a Hansel and Gretel sort of place built about 1560, and in the nineteenth century it was home to a family with fourteen children; the last member died in 1976, and is buried at Minstead. Local arts and crafts are displayed in this lovely setting, with pottery, carvings and much else, but the most unusual features are the sculptures by Maxie Lane – stools, tables and so on carved entirely without joints, in one great piece of sycamore, or wych elm. The 'biggest sculptured table in the world' is there, not one joint, eighteen feet long, and weighing nearly two tons; an extraordinary skill.

Much of the north of the forest area is bleak, undulating heathland, almost moorland, wilder and more desolate than the heath at Beaulieu. The forest's highest point is here, 414 feet above sea level. Several narrow roads cross the heath, from Cadnam to Fordingbridge, and past Bramshaw Golf Course into Wiltshire. The lovely River Avon flows to the coast along the western edge of Hampshire, sweeping deep and fast through Breamore, Fordingbridge and Ringwood, to the sea at Christchurch. All these towns are beyond the forest boundary, and strangely, their atmosphere is quite unlike any of those within.

The entrance to the busy market town of Ringwood is much changed due to the relentless advance of the motorway. The old road was severely butchered, with the total loss of a number of pink and white blossom trees that were a joy to travellers in April and May. I was saddened to see them go. Spoiled too, was the distant view of the church, a stately grey building with a high tower, on a knoll, its grounds now trimmed nearly to the walls, with the traffic hurtling closely by. The church was re-built last century, but it has retained some parts of the older place of worship.

A pleasant, bustling little town, Ringwood has a street market and as great a variety of building styles as will be found anywhere, once you look above the shop-fronts. There are many 'White Harts' about the country, but the inn near the market place lays claim to be the original.

It was to the house known as Monmouth House that the Duke of Monmouth was taken in 1685, recaptured after his flight from the Battle of Sedgemoor. He wrote a sad and remorseful letter there, in an attempt to gain a hearing with James II, the uncle he had opposed; indeed, this was granted, but it was an abject interview, and he still lost his head shortly afterwards.

Monmouth brought disaster to the Lisle family at Moyles Court, which stands on the other side of the main road from Ringwood to Fordingbridge. Two fugitives from the unsuccessful rebellion were sheltered there by the old mistress of the house, and although she protested that she was not aware of the men's politics, she was arrested and tried at the Winchester Assize. The Hampshire jury found her not guilty of the offence during two separate trials, but the ruthless Judge Jeffreys had made up his mind to make an example of her, and bullied the men into returning the verdict he required. He sentenced the old lady to be burned alive, but this the Hampshire men firmly refused to carry out, and in 1685 she was executed in Winchester, opposite what is now the City Museum.

The funeral procession wound its solemn way back to Ellingham, where she was laid to rest in the churchyard familiar to her. The pretty little church is built in attractive russet stone, with a small shingled spire and belfry. The large front porch is topped by an unusual sundial of 1720, painted gaily in blue and gold. Electricity is connected to the church, but there are masses of candles everywhere, including three very grand chandeliers of thirteenth-century brass. Unusually, the church lacks a chancel arch, a wooden screen with an old beam right across serving this purpose.

By following the river northwards (through thick blackberry country), you come to Ibsley, where at one time a small airfield, was located; later used as a race-track from time to time. In August 1978, when the site was being developed for building, an excavator scooping out the blue silty clay discovered two pieces of tusk, some eighteen feet beneath the surface. The tusk was broken by the digger, but the two pieces together measure 3½ feet, and appear to have belonged to an elephant or mammoth, wandering along the Hampshire riverside more than 100,000 years ago.

Beyond Fordingbridge, a jumbled town not built for the motor age, the county juts firmly into Wiltshire in a rather aggressive way. However, the 'peninsula' is an interesting piece of land.

Morley Hewitt, who died in 1974 at the age of 81, was a historian and archaeologist, and one of his happiest and most successful 'finds' must surely have been the Roman villa at Rockbourne. In this high and rather exposed field near the Wiltshire border in 1964, Morley Hewitt found buried the remains of a whole family's way of life – foundations of a kitchen, dining-room with mosaic floor in buff and terracotta, guest-room also with tessellated floor, baths, treasury and other rooms, 73 in all.

But more than just foundations – skilled and painstaking workers uncovered sufficient 'rubbish' to enable them to piece together a comprehensive jig-saw. The walls of the villa for instance, and probably the floors and roof, were built of stone from Purbeck and Portland; it was fitted with an efficient box-flue, drain-pipes and fittings of lead from the Mendips and Derbyshire; it had glass in its windows, which swung on hinges of iron, probably smelted on the site from local iron-stone, using shale from Kimmeridge.

The people carried pocket knives, and keys, and used the tools of stonemasons and carpenters. They kept themselves busy making pots from shale, grinding flour on a quern, sharpening dull blades on a whetstone, spinning yarn by spindle-whorl, and using fuller's earth to dress the woven cloth.

Life was not all work however, and the women pinned up their tresses with bone spikes almost identical with the 'roller-pins' that are used today; they wore brooches and rings in silver, ear-rings and bangles of gilt. Some small items indicate that the children were no less fashion conscious than their mothers. The men too, had buckles and buttons of pewter and bronze.

The Romans of Rockbourne seem to have been partial to shell-fish, for among the pots and platters of familiar red (and some black) glazed Samian ware, are countless pieces of oysters, mussels, limpets, cockles, whelks and scallops, snails too, and poultry bones, egg-shells and corn, in carbonised condition. They seem to have kept their own domestic animals, for there are bones of horse and ox, goat and ram, as well as antlers, a raven's beak and the tusk of a boar.

Money was essential even in those long-ago days, and numerous coins have been found spanning many generations of emperors, with the heads of Romans whose names are familiar – Nero, Vespasian and Hadrian – and some that are unfamiliar.

A museum was opened on the site in 1972, displaying all the uncovered relics, and gives a fascinating look at Roman life.

Visitors to Rockbourne often wonder what the monument is that they can see a field or two away, for it is on private land, and they cannot reach it. It commemorates Sir Eyre

Coote, a close associate and adviser of Clive of India; he bought an estate at Rockbourne, and although he died in India, his body was brought home to lie in the countryside he loved.

A patchwork of narrow, winding lanes will bring you to one of Hampshire's great houses, at Breamore, which the locals pronounce 'Bremmer', a charming village slumbering beside the deep Avon. Breamore House is a lovely Elizabethan Manor completed in 1583 and built of rosy brick, with masses of tall chimneys and steep gables. The Dodington family owned the house for nearly a hundred years, after which it passed, through marriage, to Robert Greville, Lord Brooke, who was later created Earl of Warwick.

In 1748, Breamore House was sold to Sir Edward Hulse, in whose family it has remained. Parts of the mansion are open to the public, who can see the paintings, ornaments and furniture collected over ten generations.

The Great Hall, panelled throughout, is the largest room, 84 feet by 21 feet, and from the tall windows there are panoramic views of the New Forest and the lush Avon Valley. Perhaps its greatest treasure is the painting by Van Dyck on the north wall, and important too, are the two Brussels tapestries, worked about 1630, a fishing scene and a harvesting scene, the latter a charming picture showing the happy faces of a village celebrating a successful 'gathering in'. The furniture in the dining-room is good solid oak, with Tudor character, and includes two early refectory tables with elaborately carved 'legs'. Portraits of the Hulse family hang in one of the drawing-rooms, and in another is a very fine Chippendale overmantel in gilt. The bedrooms have very different characters, from heavy Tudor timbers, to a dainty Georgian room with its four-poster bed hung with drapes of blue silk damask.

There is a maze in the grounds, and two museums, – with collections of carriages and of agricultural implements.

Indeed, Breamore has so much to offer, for long before William Dodington was heard of, Saxon men had built their sturdy flint-walled church near to the river. All the Saxon features are there, the long and short stones, pilaster strips and double-splayed windows, for Breamore church was built in the years around 1000, and is one of the rare almost-complete churches of that period. It is exceptionally large too, for the time, with a length of 96 feet 6 inches, and it contains Anglo-Saxon wording incised on the north face of a transept arch, something I have not seen elsewhere.

Old beams support the roof, and beneath the bell-tower in the centre hang twelve colourful coats of arms; and there are several memorials to the Hulse family. In a church of such great antiquity, there is naturally much to interest the visitor, and the Saxon rood inside the porch is especially worthy of notice, mutilated though it is.

The road eastwards passes between a loop of the Avon streams and a vast acreage of greenhouses, a business concerned with pot-plants known as 'The House of Flowers' at Wood-green. The place is being taken over by a larger enterprise and will probably change, but until now, it has been open to the public at selected times, and the mass of colour and perfume has been almost overpowering, and very beautiful.

For a mile or two, the highway skirts the Wiltshire border, then turns off eventually to the two villages of West and East Wellow, the latter a scattered parish, whose cottagers were at one time visited by Florence Nightingale.

A curving drive from the A27 leads to Embley Park, a school now, but for years the home of the Nightingale family. It was from there that its most famous member took her first steps in the career that was to make her one of the foremost women of her age.

Florence Nightingale was born in the spring of 1820, in the Italian city after which she was named; it was as fashionable then to travel in Europe as it is today, and with Napoleon firmly dealt with five years earlier, the journey could be undertaken without peril.

When the family returned to England to settle, they chose for their 'winter house', the red-brick mansion at Embley, near Romsey, with many windows and tall chimneys, se-cluded in a thickly wooded park with a wide lake. The Nightingales lived a carefree society life of ease and pleasure, and in her younger days, Florence enjoyed it all, the balls and expeditions, and the house-parties, which included some sparkling affairs at Broadlands, home of the Prime-Minister, Lord Palmerston. But she grew tired of her restricted lady's life, and fretted at not being able to do something more useful; and more important, she knew what her vocation was to be, and what was expected of her during her lifetime.

She took to visiting the cottagers in the village, taking it upon herself to tend the sick, and voicing her opinion of the systems of drainage and sanitation that affected the health of the rural community. She knew that her destiny lay in nursing and improving the administration and design of hospitals, but these tasks lay quite outside the bounds set by society; hospitals were institutions of poverty and squalor, staffed by women of small intelligence and no training, and frequently of few morals and drunken habits.

For years, her mother and her clinging, neurotic sister refused to consider letting Florence leave her comfortable home for such a purpose, and the years brought heartache and despair for all at Embley Park. But destiny will not be diverted, and with the courage and single-mindedness that were to be tried to the limit in later years, and the help of influential friends, Florence won her private battle, with far-reaching results.

Her full and extraordinary life ended in 1910, when she was ninety. In the days of bitter frustration, Florence prayed in the little twelfth-century church of East Wellow to the God who had called her, and under the beeches of a Hampshire hillside is the family tomb in which she lies. A simple monument marks her grave, with just her initials "F.N." and the dates of her life "Born 12th May 1820, Died 13th August 1910".

The church is full of interest on its own account, including remnants of medieval wall-paintings, and one of the country's oldest bells, dated 1420; but it is for Florence Nightingale that many pilgrims come. In the porch hangs an octagonal lamp, said to be the field-lamp 'the lady' carried on the weary night-rounds, when the cramped rows of sick men and wounded kissed her shadow as it passed, and there are other personal items which belonged to that truly remarkable woman, so many years ahead of her time.

As the A27 heads eastward towards Romsey, a lay-by on the left gives the first glimpse of the old abbey, set in the green valley among the trees.

X

ROMSEY

Sparkling waters and frothy blossoms are the hallmarks of Romsey in springtime. This jumbled old town is built around the many streams of the River Test, flowing south from the downs of north Hampshire to Southampton Water. In May, this part of the A27 is flanked by white blossom trees, and after the first puff of wind, it is as though snow had fallen, the delicate petals showering down in great drifts. And so it is in the Memorial Park just north of the main road, where the river swirls along three of its four sides. It is a most pleasant place, with chestnut boughs dipping into the water, and pink and white blossom all around; the banks are edged with daffodils and wallflowers, and numbers of mallard families make their homes there. The park was opened in 1920, a lovely memorial to the men who died in the long war; a great field gun stands by the entrance, its twin not far away on a gravelled forecourt of Broadlands, the neighbouring estate.

Salmon is the fish of the lower Test, and the 'salmon leap' at the weir of Sadlers Mill, beyond the park, is an annual attraction for residents and visitors alike, when the great silver fish return in November and December from their travels abroad, leaping high against the tumbling water to lay their eggs in the river of their birth.

It is only a short walk along The Meads to the Square, which is the hub of Romsey; there is a pleasantly 'backwoods' atmosphere to the little town, that is particularly noticeable here. Like all good market squares, it has a statue, a bronze figure of one of Romsey's leading nineteenth-century residents, Lord Palmerston, sculpted by Matthew Noble, and standing on a high plinth of pink-mottled granite. The third Lord Palmerston was born at Broadlands, and loved to return there to relax from the burden of his duties as Prime Minister to Queen Victoria. He looks eastward, towards the handsome

Corn Exchange of 1864, built just a year before he died, and now used by Barclays Bank. On one side of the Square is the bow-windowed 'Dolphin'; on the other, the 'White Horse', three storeys and attics above, bright with window-boxes of geraniums.

Along Bell Street and through the Square in 1100. Purkis the charcoal-burner trundled the body of Willam Rufus, the king, from his sudden death in the New Forest to the capital at Winchester. And just visible above the rooftops is the abbey, sturdy and seemingly eternal. If the Square is the hub of Romsey, the abbey is its heart, beating for a thousand years in this lush valley. There is no soaring spire; the building is bulky and squat, with only a low tower, but its presence is immense.

It was Edward, eldest son of Alfred the Great who built the first church at Romsey in 907, a simple affair, of wood maybe, or wattle. Archbishop Dunstan of Canterbury took an interest with Ethelwold, Bishop of Winchester, and soon a Benedictine order of nuns flourished. Edward's own daughter, Alfred's grandchild, may have been the first Abbess and she is buried there.

All round the coasts however, the Scandinavians were rampaging through town and country, with no respect for religious communities. Hampshire suffered badly in the years round the turn of that century; in 1004 the nuns fled to the safety of Winchester's walls, and almost surely their abbey was ruined. But in time, the women returned and a new church was started, in stone this time, and larger, with more extensive conventual buildings. Two large stone carvings from this early church can be seen in today's abbey, one outside on the west-facing wall of the south transept, with the 'hand of God' above, and the other inside in the south choir aisle, above the altar.

The present church bears the lengthy dedication of St Mary and St Ethelflaeda, after the Blessed Virgin and one of Romsey's best-loved Abbesses; it was begun in the first quarter of the twelfth century, and continued to serve the educational needs of young noblewomen. Even Scotland's monarchs, Malcolm and Margaret, sent their two daughters to Romsey Abbey to be taught by their aunt, Christina, a nun already resident there.

In common with other old churches, the Norman abbey has seen much alteration over the centuries, until in 1539, with Henry VIII on England's throne, the community was dissolved and the estate split up. An abbey steward bought the part we know as Broadlands, and the church was sold to its parishioners for £100. The deed of sale remains in Romsey's possession.

It is a cool, restful place, but for such a small town it is a great parish church to maintain, with a total length of 263 feet; the octagon above the tower houses a fine peal of eight bells and, inside, beneath the barrel roof, are the fat pillars and rounded arches to be expected in a Norman building. I like especially the two arches behind the High Altar, with a rather lovely bas-relief by Martin Travers between them, showing Mary and the Child.

The most elaborate monument must be the St Barbe family tomb in the south transept; the St Barbes owned Broadlands for nearly two hundred years, until 1723. Near to the tomb lies the sleeping figure of an unknown thirteenth-century woman, under a canopy of later date. There have been various suggestions about her identity, but it has not been established, which seems rather sad. There are tablets to Lord Palmerston's memory on the west wall, but he is buried in Westminster Abbey.

During restoration work undertaken in 1975, workers found, in a sealed hole, remains of what was thought to be a rose, and the discovery received much publicity. It was subsequently found to be the outer scales and fibrous roots of a bulb of the Liliaceae family. A new botanical sample was sealed away in its place, with an explanation of the circumstances, for future generations to find.

There are a number of old houses in Romsey, all within easy walking distance, sixteenth- and seventeenth-century buildings of brick with overhanging timbered upper storeys, and thatched wood-framed cottages. The oldest of them all is known as King John's House, across Church Street from the abbey, and tucked away along a gravel path. There has been much controversy over the date of this house, some sticking firmly to the opinion that it was indeed built about 1206 as a hunting box for the king. Certainly King John had a hunting lodge built in Romsey, but whether or not this was it, will I think, remain a mystery forever unsolved. However, even the

The Knightwood Oak

Breamore Church

Breamore House

Romsey from the
Salisbury road

River Test near
Broadlands, Romsey

'King John's Hunting
Lodge', Romsey

Broadlands

Modern and Ancient: Chilbolton Observatory and Quarley bells

Wherwell

Drovers' House, Stockbridge

Fisherman's hut, River Test at Longstock

Whitchurch Silk Mill

sceptics allow that the house was built before 1240.

The first floor consisted of a large open hall which would have been used for general domestic purposes, and was un-connected by any internal stair from the ground floor. In an upper room, the walls have a number of pictures and writing scratched on them, confirmation, if any were needed, that the defacing of walls is not a pastime peculiar to the twentieth century. There are shields and mottoes of noblemen of six hundred years ago, and an amateurish portrait of a man who appears to be Edward I, similar to the head and coronet seen on coins between 1302 and 1310. Who drew them, I wonder? Page-boys perhaps, left behind to clear up after their masters' carousing, themselves maybe a little the worse for Romsey ale?

John Foster, who had bought Broadlands after the dis-solution of the abbey, later sold the bigger house and bought this one, together with the Tudor cottage next door, its walls bulging now. The document of conveyance, dated 17th July 1571, is on show in the house. Foster was married to Jane Wadhams, who had been a nun, and was a niece of Jane Seymour. Another famous document, the charter granted to Romsey by King James I in 1607, is also on display, but in photograph form, the original being kept safely in the Town Hall.

The old pair of houses are much altered now, but some of the original beams were replaced after restoration work was carried out, and there are two great fireplaces up and down stairs. The buildings have been put to various uses over the years, and are open to the public as a museum for the area.

My early recollections of railway embankment hoardings advertising the 'Strong Country' come home to roost in Romsey, for a brewery has stood on the Horsefair site at the end of Church Street, at least since the sixteenth century, and maybe earlier, when, depending on the location, one penny could buy up to four gallons of good strong ale. Romsey has quite a reputation to live down, for there was a time when, if a man had imbibed so much liquor that his legs could no longer support him, he was said to be "so drunk, he must have been to Romsey".

The old brewery was leased to Thomas Strong in 1858, together with twenty-three licensed houses, and was later sold to him. Nearly thirty years later, the name of David Faber was important to the firm. Faber, with brothers who were to become better known in banking and publishing circles, had a shrewd business head; on acquiring the Horsefair Brewery, he immediately bought out the two competitors in nearby Bell Street and The Hundred, and soon afterwards, others at Weyhill and Christchurch. Before the end of the century, Strong's of Romsey was turned into a limited company, one of the biggest names in Hampshire brewing.

Strong's continued to expand, taking control of more and more smaller businesses, including, in 1965, Mew, Langton & Co. Ltd. By this time, Whitbreads were represented on Strong's board, and in 1969 the two giants merged to become Whitbread Wessex Ltd, to their mutual advantage.

One of the reasons for Strong's great success was its water, drawn from its own wells, and particularly suited to the making of beer. The brewery is still at Horsefair, at the junction of Church Street and Mill Lane, employing some 550 staff, and its distribution area extends as far as Bordon, Basingstoke, Wilton and Christchurch. Manufacturing techniques have changed greatly over the years; I wonder how the beer compares?

The Test streams flow beneath Mill Lane, where two mills were recorded in the Domesday Book, Burnt Mill and Mead Mill, originally fulling mills it is believed, but put to a number of uses over the centuries.

In the early 1960s, Donald Baker brought the derelict properties with the intention of fishing, and maybe dabbling in farming. The water looped around green tongues of land, and the new owner realised the potential of this ideal setting. With hard work and vision, he reclaimed the neglected farmland, and turned one and a half picturesque acres into a commercial water-garden. The main land is used for grazing and crops, and he grows and sells water-plants.

In 1971, the Sounding Arch on the Embley Park Estate was demolished in the cause of road widening, and some of the stone was used to make a wishing well for charity in the gardens. The well was opened in July that year by Lord Mountbatten, with the words "God bless her and all who wish in her".

On the road east from Romsey, the long, brick 'mile wall' is a well-known landmark which ends with a timbered lodge guarding one of the entrances to Broadlands, home of Admiral of the Fleet, Earl Mountbatten of Burma. The gravel drive winds between pasture and woodland, the haunt of hares and pheasants, and spattered in late spring by mists of bluebells. The portico front of the house can be glimpsed through the trees, with the gleam of the River Test beyond.

Broadlands is a very special house, not in appearance perhaps, but in character and in its associations. Add the tremendous personality of its owner, and the combination is unique. The atmosphere is very much that of a 'man's house', but it is none the worse for that, and His Lordship loves it dearly.

The estate was once a part of Romsey Abbey, and links forged a thousand years ago are still strong. The house was built in 1536 and when, shortly afterwards, the abbey was surrendered, the acres known as 'Brodelandes' were separated and sold to one of its stewards, John Foster. Sir Francis Fleming bought the property, and then it was sold again to the St Barbe family, in whose possession it remained for nearly two hundred years. During that time, in 1607, James I stayed with Edward St Barbe at Broadlands when he granted Romsey its first charter, and he planted two mulberry trees in the grounds to commemorate the occasion. The trees still flourish, and three more were planted near them three hundred and fifty years later, on 6th April 1957, two by Her Majesty Queen Elizabeth, and one by Prince Philip. There are other 'special' trees too, over two hundred, including copper beeches planted by the Duke and Duchess of Windsor.

When Broadlands was sold again in 1736, the buyer was Henry Temple, who had been created Lord Palmerston for his political achievements. His son predeceased him, and his grandson, another Henry, inherited the estate and the title in 1757.

The second Viscount cared deeply about Broadlands, and spent much time and money making improvements which altered the whole appearance of the house, and favoured the Palladian style. He was also a lover of the arts, and brought to his home many of the treasures that are there today, gathered from his travels abroad. He numbered Reynolds and Swift among his friends also Garrick and Sheridan. A formidable quartet used their skills to beautify the house and grounds – the talented Henry Holland, Lancelot (Capability) Brown,

Robert Adam and Josiah Wedgwood. The Wedgwood Room is still decorated in the familiar blue and white, and the considerable collection of Wedgwood pieces dates from that time. The newest piece is a large plaque of Lord Mountbatten's head in profile, made in 1978, and taken from a fine portrait by Ben Schwartz.

Henry John Temple was born at Broadlands in October 1784 and, like his father, he was only seventeen when he became (the third) Viscount Palmerston. A bachelor until middle age, he also made politics his career, becoming Foreign Secretary, and then Prime Minister. In 1839 he married his life's love, Emily Cowper, who had been widowed by the death of Earl Cowper. The affair caused a considerable stir and was the subject of much drawing-room tittle-tattle, especially as he left Broadlands to her second son, who became the first Lord Mount Temple. He it was who built the three-storey bachelor's wing, which was used as a hostel during the last war, but was pulled down in 1954.

In due course, the lovely old house was inherited by Wilfrid Ashley, son of Evelyn Ashley, and great-grandson of Lady Palmerston; he too loved Broadlands, and brought his bride, Maud Cassels, there. Their first daughter, Edwina, was born there in 1901.

A year earlier, at Frogmore House, Windsor, a fourth child had been born to Prince Louis of Battenberg and his wife, Victoria, named after her royal grandmother. The child was a son, also called Louis, and like his father, he made his career in the Royal Navy. In 1917, the family changed their name; Prince Louis was created Marquess of Milford Haven, and his youngest son became Lord Louis Mountbatten; five years later the young officer married Edwina Ashley, and thus began one of the most spectacular and rewarding partnerships of our time. Sadly, 'Lady Louis' died in 1960, while working with the Red Cross in Borneo.

During the second half of the nineteenth century, Broadlands was the graceful background for a dazzle of social gatherings, with balls, parties and banquets making for much gaiety. The Palmerstons were hosts to monarchs, governors, statesmen and their ladies; fine gowns rustled beneath glittering tiaras and medals, stars and orders gleamed under the chandeliers. Florence Nightingale, in her butterfly heyday, dined and danced there, visiting from her home nearby.

Broadlands is scarcely less busy today, and Lord Mountbatten lives his life in a whirl of activity despite the advancing years. "I would rather wear out than rust," he says cheerfully. The entertaining goes on, less lavishly perhaps, but without doubt, few other houses in England have so exalted a guest-list, and there is a book kept in which the signature of every visitor who stays overnight is entered.

Lord Mountbatten's years of distinguished service in war (and peacetime too) are a story in themselves, and he loves to gather together friends he made during that time, and to talk, as men will, of the days of excitement and comradeship, recalling anecdotes and characters of mutual interest. "I am the only one left," he says, with a certain satisfaction, "all the other war leaders are dead – Churchill, Roosevelt, Stalin, and the great commanders, they've all gone now."

'Lord Louis' is a legend; and so is Broadlands. The 5,800-acre estate provides one of the best pheasant shoots in the country, and the wide ribbon of chalk river, with luscious salmon and trout, flows close to the house. Nearly a quarter of the grounds are woodland, and with his grandson and heir, the Honourable Norton Knatchbull, His Lordship farms 2,000 acres. The estate is a haven of peace and tranquillity. Kitchen gardens and greenhouses growing exotic fruits lie to the north of the house, together with the much-used stables, built in the reign of William III, with their original round and oval mullioned windows.

Inside the cool house, precious Greek marbles line the hall, brought there by the second Lord Palmerston, and the collection includes a rather beautiful *Boy on a Dolphin*, a copy by Nollekens of the work by Michelangelo, now housed in a museum in Leningrad.

The state-rooms are spacious and elegant; each contains a fireplace in the familiar Adam style, and the ceilings are gilded, with delicate paintings by Angelica Kauffman adding charm in the drawing-room. Little has changed in two centuries; when the blue curtains hanging at the long windows needed renewing in 1860, they were rewoven on the original matrix and loom, and in the same materials, and Lady Mountbatten had them rewoven again in the same way in 1950.

Treasures are everywhere, huge Van Dycks in the drawing-room, Canalettos and portraits by Lely; a self-portrait by Reynolds hangs on one wall, a winsome picture of Emma Hart, later to become Lady Hamilton, on another. Busts, price-less paintings, Dresden china, rare books and signed photo-graphs of the world's leaders abound in every room. There are mementoes and gifts spanning the centuries, a small ewer and basin of fine porcelain for instance, a possession of Marie Antoinette, Queen of France at the time of her execution in 1792, which Josephine Beauharnais gave Lord Palmerston a few days before her marriage to Napoleon Bonaparte.

There are ivories from India and Burma, and from China a curved tusk, some four feet long and much carved, with a grinning mandarin as the central figure. Over the fireplace in the library hangs a great equestrian portrait of the third Vis-count, and on the table is an intricately carved replica of King Theebaw's Lion Throne, a gift of thanks from the Government of Burma when Lord Mountbatten was Viceroy of India.

Family photographs stand on every surface, our own Royal Family, the King and Queen of Sweden, Spain, Greece, and Thailand, Prince Rainier and Princess Grace of Monaco, Roosevelt, Eisenhower and Nehru – relatives and friends the world over. In the corridors lined with plaques and pictures, are paintings by Montague Dawson, of Lord Mountbatten's badly listing destroyer, H.M.S. *Kelly*, torpedoed in May 1940, and limping back to port under heavy air attack with star-board gunwale awash. In pride of place is a trophy of war, the *Kelly*'s tattered white ensign, flown in this action.

Trophies of a more peaceful kind, showing prowess on the polo field, are packed tightly on eight shelves of an enormous cabinet. There is an original spiral oak staircase linking the three storeys. The main staircases are lined with sixteenth-century family portraits, ancestors of the present earl, who are shared by his great-nephew, the Prince of Wales, and four ancestors who married Tsars of Russia. There are medals and coins, swords, kukris, daggers and kris, and yet another – the mightiest – trophy of war, a Japanese sword of 1292, handed to Lord Mountbatten as a token of surrender at Saigon on 30th November 1945, the victorious conclusion of a long and difficult campaign.

Broadlands has its own cinema in the sixteenth-century oak

room, where guests are entertained, and also the estate staff and their families. Grandeur old and new are linked even there, for the Baltic oak panelling was installed by the old St Barbe family, while two modern chairs are from Carnaervon, where they were used at the Investiture of the Prince of Wales in 1969.

The newly married Princess Elizabeth and Prince Philip spent the first part of their honeymoon at Broadlands, and for the Queen the lovely house remains a place of sanctuary. Indeed, the Portico Room is used by Her Majesty whenever she visits, and it is without doubt the most feminine room in the house, cool but cosy, with chintzy curtains and a canopied four-poster bed.

Broadlands has always been a mecca for the world's most influential people, and at a desk in the corner of the drawing-room frequently sits one of the most influential of them all, Earl Mountbatten of Burma. His desk is set at an angle, so that one window overlooks the formal gardens and fountain, and the other, green lawns sweeping down to the river. His Lordship has decided to open his house to the public in 1979.

I hope the decision does not destroy for ever the mystery and tranquillity that is the very essence of the charm of Broadlands, but there is no doubt that many people will want to see the historic house that is still so much a home, and to share its treasures. It is a house certainly, that I shall never tire of visiting.

XI

THE NORTH-WEST

The A27 takes motorists past the old village of Chilworth, with its Norman church containing two bells thought to be the oldest in Hampshire. The area has been thoroughly spoiled in the 1970s, due to road alterations connected with the M27, and much building of residential accommodation for the University of Southampton.

The road leads on through Chandler's Ford and Hursley, and in these lanes, quite early on most mornings, it is not unusual to see a coach and four bowling along. For each day, the head groom from Cranbury Park at Otterbourne takes this equipage out for an airing, a picturesque sight. It is a sight much in keeping with the village of Hursley, which has spread certainly, but not unattractively. The main street is still hedged with higgledy-piggledy terraced houses with timbered fronts, steep jutting gables above quaint windows, and of course, the tall chimneys which are a feature of the village, craftsmen-built stacks, all different, and patterned with intricate designs. Frank New of the 'Fox and Hounds' at Beauworth fashioned some of them, but others are much older. Some are tucked away and have to be looked for, but the best-known example is the triple chimney topping a cottage on the main road, near the ivied walls of the 'King's Head'.

Hursley will always be associated with its nineteenth-century vicar, John Keble, who preached a generation of sermons in the fine grey stone church, with its tall lancet windows and low tower. He also wrote *The Christian Year*, a popular work of his time. He retired to Bournemouth because of his wife's ill-health, and they both died there within the year, in 1866. There are memorials to him in the church, but a more useful tribute stands on the outskirts of the village, the John Keble Memorial School.

There is a monument to Richard Cromwell too, for

Oliver's unambitious son married Dorothy Maijor of Hursley Park in the church on 1st May 1649. Richard failed to follow in the footsteps of his ruthless father, and was happier being 'Tumbledown Dick', countryman.

The mounds of Farley Mount, rising behind Hursley, are a favourite picnic spot, undulating land, thick with woods. This used to be riding country, and a tall stone monument tells how, in 1733, a horse and rider came unexpectedly to the brink of a deep chalk pit. Too late to avoid it, the pair did the only possible thing – carried on into a gigantic leap, and the splendid horse carried his master safely across the great chasm.

Countryside and farming are subjects never far away in Hampshire, but the business of teaching these skills had in the past been confined to the passing of knowledge from father to son, a satisfactory enough system, but limited. The need for formal agricultural education was recognised long ago, and the idea gathered momentum after a professor was appointed to Edinburgh University in 1790, to instruct students in that subject.

In Hampshire, such schooling started in 1891, with a series of travelling horse-drawn vans touring the villages in the county, giving lectures, lantern shows and demonstrations. A permanent farm-school was set up at Old Basing at the turn of the century, sixty-one green acres "to provide instruction in the science and practice of agriculture and gardening . . . and . . . a centre for domestic work in the County".

There was only one snag to the site at Old Basing; the land was leased from the estate of Lord Bolton, whose great interest of raising pheasants proved a considerable hazard to young farmers trying to raise cabbages. One fresh green patch of succulent young plants disappeared entirely. A new location was sought. In the autumn of 1914, the school moved to its own land, unharried by game-hunting gentry, at Sparsholt, north of Hursley.

The College of Agriculture has grown in size, scope and status since them, with residential quarters and leisure rooms, laboratories, conference halls, machinery workshops and green-houses. Most of the courses are full-time, but there are some for days and evenings. The syllabus is comprehensive; general agriculture, dairy, pigs, arable, management, game-keeping, water-keeping and fish-farming, agricultural engineering, horticulture, poultry and also bee-keeping – with 100 colonies, it is the largest such department in any college in England or Wales. Rural home economics are taught as well as two dozen or so crafts from dressmaking and painting to spinning and cookery.

But this north-western corner of Hampshire belongs essentially to the Test Valley, with one of the most famous and coveted trout rivers in the world flowing through its heart. It would be easy to eulogise about the Test, for its scenery, its verdure and the villages along its course are very beautiful.

So, no doubt, thought a group of Augustinian monks, who chose the lush riverside to build their priory at·Mottisfont, a little north of Romsey, in 1201. Three centuries later, when the priory was dissolved, it was given to Lord Sandys, who left his larger home at The Vyne after the expensive Civil War. Mottisfont had been a gift from Henry VIII, in exchange for the villages of Chelsea and Paddington.

The house is a soft, grey, mellow place, even the name is in keeping; the Sandys family had it rebuilt, incorporating parts of the old priory, and it stands gracefully between smooth green lawns and massive, age-old beeches, intermingled with cedars, planes and chestnuts.

In the church there are some interesting medieval features, and some lovely fifteenth- and sixteenth-century stained-glass windows. Perhaps the most splendid part of the old buildings is the thirteenth-century monks' cellarium, a great cool room, where round Norman pillars,· undamaged by time, support a vast vaulted roof.

The American artist, Rex Whistler, spent some time at Mottisfont, and in 1938 he covered one of the rooms, walls and ceiling, with delicate paintings, including, in an alcove, his famous 'Smoking Urn'. In 1957, the house was given to the National Trust, and the cellarium and The Whistler Room are now opened regularly to the public.

One of the many pretty thatched villages through which the Test flows is Kings Somborne, a manor held by John of Gaunt, Duke of Lancaster, in the fourteenth century.

But the 'capital' of the Test Valley is Stockbridge, heart of the fishing country, a busy little town with a single broad main street. It was busier still at the turn of the century, when the Turf was as much in vogue there as the river, and

Stockbridge Races were a major event in the sporting calendar. This interest has declined now, but the ivy-covered grandstand on Danebury Down remains, and the stables at Chattis Hill are still in business. A devoted follower of the Danebury meeting was King Edward VII, who lodged in the town for the duration of the races, staying at Hermit Lodge, just off the main street opposite the church.

Across the lane from Hermit Lodge stands a more modest lodging, the Drovers' House. Its wall has been altered to allow for the insertion of a much-needed window, but it is a pity that it was so placed, for it interrupts the large painted lettering of great antiquity – "Gwiar Tymherus Porfa Flasus Cwrw Da Gwaltan Cyrsurus" – an old time, melodic version of the modern "B & B, H & C and Car Space". For long ago, sheep-drovers trekked the long journey with their flocks, from the windswept hills of Wales to the sheep-fairs of Hampshire, and they stayed at this old thatched house overnight. The ancient words were for their benefit, and offered the shepherds 'Seasoned Hay, Tasty Pastures, Good Beer, Comfortable Beds'.

Tom Cannon was the great name of Stockbridge racing, being owner, trainer and jockey. He owned the imposing seventeenth-century Grosvenor Hotel in the main street, known the world over; but its fame nowadays is in fishing circles, for at Tom Cannon's death in 1917, the hotel was bought by that most exclusive of angling groups, the Houghton Fishing Club. The hotel is their headquarters, with rooms set aside solely for their use. The River Test is reputedly the finest trout stream of its kind in the world, fed as it is by clear springs under the chalk soil. Anglers come from all continents to fish there. The Houghton Club shares its fourteen miles of fishing between the twenty-two fortunate members, and the club-spirit is very important to them, giving a close-knit atmosphere quite different from the usual syndicates to whom river-fishing is big business. The Houghton is the oldest dry-fly fishing club in the world, with a continuous record of every fish caught, by whom, and on what fly, since its foundation in 1822.

These delicate flies are fashioned during the winter months by the fishery manager, Mick Lunn, whose nimble fingers twist feather and hair into Ginger Quills, Black and Golds, Houghton Rubies, a local favourite, and the unique Lunn's

Particular. For Mick Lunn is a third-generation water-bailiff, and his grandfather created and perfected his own special fly.

The Houghton Club has its own trout fishery to ensure good stocks of the native brown trout, and rainbow, originally from North America, which after more that thirty years has adapted successfully and become 'naturalised'. The trout spawn in November, when the eggs are taken from them and kept in the hatchery. After six weeks the eggs hatch, and are nurtured and fed on nutritional pelleted food (much cleaner to handle than the knackered meat of yester-year) till their second year, when they are turned into the river, or sold to other dealers.

Roads radiate in all directions from Stockbridge, north to Andover, eastwards towards Winchester, and west to the Wallops, and to Danebury, where the race-meetings were held.

Men of the Iron Age built a hill fort at Danebury more than two thousand years ago. Archaeologists continue to show a great interest in the site, which is considered to be one of the best examples of its kind in the country. It is a place of pleasure now, and so popular with walkers that one is rarely alone there.

By the time you reach the Wallops, a series of villages with the strange names of Nether Wallop, Over Wallop and so on, you are nearly into Wiltshire. Wood anemones line the lanes there, succeeding clouds of old-man's beard and catkins, with the brilliant orange berries of lords and ladies brightening the verges in late summer; willows grow in profusion there too, and it is said that W. G. Grace would only have his cricket bats made from the willows of Wallop.

Sometimes, the un-English sounds of lions roaring and elephants trumpeting can be heard there too as Mary Chipperfield goes about her business of animal-training on her small farm. It was early in the 1600s that William Chipperfield brought his performing bear from France to entertain the English crowds; they must have enjoyed the act, for the name has become synonymous over the centuries with the circus world.

In 1955, Jimmy Chipperfield left the Big Top to farm the family land at Middle Wallop, but returned to the wild animal circuit five years later when he opened the small zoo at

Southampton. An idea was forming in his mind, the first concept of the safari-park. In 1966, the original of such parks was opened under his aegis at the Wiltshire estate of Longleat, seat of the Marquis of Bath, and since then many others are flourishing throughout the world. With film-making, safari-parks, zoos and circuses, the twentieth-century Chipperfields are big business; a far cry from William and his performing bear.

Across the old Roman track from Silchester to the settlements of Old Sarum and beyond, rises yet another earth-work on Quarley Hill, probably of older date even than Danebury. The Domesday Book, a modern work compared to the hill fort, talks of four ploughlands and a church in the demesne of Quarley. That was in 1086, and ploughlands there are still, and a church too, on the same site if not wholly the same building.

Today's flint walls are nearly a yard thick; the tiny interior seats only fifty parishioners, and is well cared for and alive, brightened always with fresh flowers. A small organ is pumped quite adequately with foot-bellows. Much of the church's fabric dates from the twelfth century, with additions during successive centuries, and preserved there are records of baptisms and burials since 1559. Perhaps Quarley's most unusual feature is its bells. A casual observer may think that it has none, for the sloping red-tiled roof has neither tower nor steeple to contain a belfry. But outside, behind the north wall, St Michael's bells hang under their own shelter, nearly shoulder high; three large bells, played by hand, their rims skimming the ground as they swing to and fro. The inscription on one tells that Henry Paulet, sixteenth Marquis of Winchester, had the bell recast in 1905.

The name of Paulet crops up wherever you go in Hampshire. After the sacking of Basing House, the Paulet family moved west to make their home at the village of Amport, in a house that now belongs to the R.A.F. Many are the tales that persist in this rural community about the famous old family in their midst, whose failings, according to the locals, were immorality and curiosity; eighty-five natural Paulets were scattered around the neighbourhood at one time, so they say. They were intrepid horsemen too, and the fifteenth Marquis, Augustus John Paulet, was a familiar sight, driving his teams of red and blue roans around the lanes, four-in-hand.

It was this Augustus John, who, according to tradition, sought to redress the family honour by righting the ignominy of their crest; for the long and gruelling siege of Basing House was ended by the traitorous conduct of one of the Paulet family, bringing defeat and disaster to the Royalist cause. Thereafter, the three swords which had been pointing upwards, were turned shamefully down.

Augustus John Paulet became a major in the Coldstream Guards, and went to fight in the Boer War; but the curiosity inbred in him was his downfall, says village gossip, for when a comrade told him that there was a sniper over the ridge, the major stood up to ask "Where?", and was promptly sniped! True or false, I do not know. Certainly he met his death in that war, and a stone memorial to him stands at the corner of Sarsen Lane and the A303. This junction has long been the cross-roads of ancient track-ways, with new names replacing the more romantic Gold Road, and Tin Road, when Irish Gold was carted from Holyhead, and tin from the mines of Cornwall; gypsy vardoes gathered in Sarsen Lane, for this was the road where flocks from Salisbury and Dorchester were driven to the Weyhill Fair. As in other parts of Hampshire, wool was the prime commodity of trade and prosperity, and Weyhill was the sheep mecca; drovers from all over the south brought their flocks, rare breeds now, some of them.

Thomas Hardy knew all about Weyhill Fair, and used the setting in his *Mayor of Casterbridge*; it appears there as Weydon-Priors in Upper Wessex, the market where Michael Henchard sold his wife to a sailor for the sum of £5. But the fair was trading long before Thomas Hardy knew it, possibly even in the days when Quarley and Danebury were thriving communities; certainly it was well established in 1225. Like so many pockets of history however, the fair died out in the middle of this century.

Reg Smith is the grandson of one of the carter's boys at the old fair, and he did not like the idea of the ancient breeds of animals dying out for ever. So in 1966, he opened a park whose aims were to preserve and breed European livestock which face this danger, and to educate young people in the ways of wildlife and country matters. It seems to be working too, for I saw a group of noisy schoolboys passing by an enclosure where an owl sat with its eyes closed, and one of them 'hushed' the others, saying "It's asleep, we mustn't wake it up."

The Weyhill European Wildlife Park and Countryside Museum provides an enjoyable outing for the family, for there are no fierce animals to alarm the nervous, and the cages are set out informally; you might at any time find a bantam, or a heron wandering across your path, for they stroll and fly at will. There are geese and otters, wildcats, red squirrels, deer, buzzards and rabbits – and donkey rides. Reg Smith is especially interested in the ancient strains of sheep and poultry, and in breeding birds of prey for his own pleasure; he has been successful with eagle owls and snowies, and also kestrels and barn owls which he releases in the wild, his contribution, he says, to the balance of nature.

The animals least familiar in the park (which costs £80 a day to run) are Barbary apes, and a pair of brown bears, not found wild in Great Britain since the tenth century. The bears produced a cub during the late winter of 1977, which the family christened Honey; they used to play with the infant, but when it was five months old the games became too hazardous, and Honey's teeth too sharp. Reg Smith encourages school parties, and is always ready to chat with his visitors, who can learn a great deal from him. He is a most interesting and knowledgeable man, with a vast store of anecdotes about the area in which he has spent his life.

On either side of the River Test just north of Stockbridge are the parishes of Lockford and Longstock, where much of the land is privately owned by the John Lewis Partnership. These banks, too, are an angler's paradise, and set on small islands in mid-stream are several picturesque fishing-huts with thatched, conical roofs, and eel-traps stretching from one side to the other. At Longstock Park, a water-garden has been created, and is open sometimes for public pleasure. It is similar to Exbury, with heathers and azaleas and other shrubs, and with wide lakes full of huge golden fish. I should like to see waterfalls for extra interest, but it is a very pleasant place, and was the idea of John Spedan Lewis, the late chairman and founder of the company.

A most alien sight in this green valley is the great saucer-shaped radio-wave reflector of Chilbolton Observatory, standing stark against the sky-line of the open downs. The former Chilbolton Airfield was chosen after a careful nationwide search for a suitable site on which to build the observatory. This radio and space research station is one of the establishments of the Science Research Council, a body formed in 1965, with a budget of £37 million a year at its disposal.

The job of the men at Chilbolton is to find out more about the structure of the Earth's atmosphere and interplanetary space, and to obtain information required by those concerned with satellite and radio communication systems. Radio tests were first carried out there in 1967, using the huge 'steerable aerial' that dwarfs the station buildings. The dish of the radio-telescope, with its intricate and web-like backing of steel, is 82 ft (25 m) in diameter, and was constructed to an accuracy of one tenth of an inch.

The precision of Chilbolton is a long way in both time and technology from the old village of Wherwell, straggling a mile or so north. I am never sure how to pronounce Wherwell; some say it should be said as 'Hurrell', and others say 'Wurrell'. However, the appearance of the village causes no controversy, for it must rank as one of the prettiest in the county, with colourful gardens, well-tended, white-washed cottages with steep thatch, mature trees and timbered terraces, and the Test streams flowing through.

The Saxon queen, Elfrida, founded a priory at Wherwell in 986, a gesture of remorse for the evil she did eight years earlier; for Elfrida was the mother of Ethelred, and her stepson Edward was on England's throne. She was a jealous woman, and ambitious for her son, and in 978, at Corfe Castle in Dorset, she arranged for the murder of the 18-year-old king, setting up Ethelred in his place. Only Ethelred did not want to be king, and made a sad botch of the job. With Tudor thoroughness, the priory was later destroyed, but odd bits and pieces can still be seen in walls around the big house built on the site. Lord De La Warr lived in the house in the sixteenth century, and later founded the state of Delaware in America. The Countess of Brecknock is the present owner.

This north-western corner of Hampshire is not populous, and Andover is its biggest town. Like Basingstoke, Andover has seen much change since an agreement with the Greater London Council in 1961, and new industrial premises, shopping centres and housing estates have now altered the face of this old country town.

The Test's main northern tributary flows by the west side of the town, the River Anton, from which Andover gets its name, which in Celtic is said to mean 'Spring Water'. Henry II granted the borough its Charter in 1178, since when it dozed through the centuries in contentment until the coaching era woke it from its slumbers, for Andover was a natural overnight stop on the long road from London to Exeter.

The parish church of St Mary stands high on a hill in the centre of the town, its pinnacled tower a considerable landmark. It was built in 1842, replacing a Norman building, and is mainly perpendicular in style.

The airspace west of Andover is often filled with the putter of small engines, and the sight of aircraft with a glider trailing behind it, is common. Then the tow-wire drops and the two craft separate, the one to enjoy a silent hour on the wind, the other to return to Thruxton Airfield for its next task.

The name of Thruxton must bring back many memories to veteran fliers of the Second World War, the gallant band of men flying the old Blenheims and Airspeed Oxfords in the early, anxious days of the 1940s. The airfield was hastily built as an annexe, first to R.A.F. Andover, and then to Netheravon. It was used for the training of bomber pilots and their navigators in the use of radio equipment enabling them to pinpoint targets in the endless night-raids across the Channel.

Later in the war, Thruxton became much involved with the Airborne Divisions, towing gliders and dropping airborne troops behind enemy lines. The unit had its share of casualties, and many were lost.

Times are happier now at Thruxton, not more peaceful, as residents will be quick to confirm, but happier. In 1968 the old airfield became the new home of the British Automobile Racing Club, after their Goodwood track was closed. With a circuit length of 2·356 miles, Thruxton comes second only to Silverstone as the fastest motor-racing track in Great Britain, the lap record standing at the beginning of 1979 at 1 minute 10.41 seconds. It is the venue each year of various European Championships and Formula 1, 2 and 3 meetings, together with motor-cycle Grands Prix and scrambles.

The debt to the men of an earlier Thruxton is not forgotten

however, and an annual air display is held on a date near to D-Day.

These high downs make ideal horse-country, and at neighbouring Fyfield and away to the north at Kingsclere, the Balding brothers have their racing-stables. The family are well-known trainers, and here at Fyfield was groomed for stardom Highland Wedding, winner of the Grand National in 1969; great were the village celebrations that evening. Toby Balding has been in the business for more than twenty years, starting at the old stables at Weyhill which were owned by Colonel Whitbread; they were sold in 1958 and are derelict now, a terrible waste of property, but at least the extensive gallops are still used.

The competition world is represented here too, namely at Appleshaw, across the main road to the west, where Lucinda Prior-Palmer has lived all her energetic young life. Before she was twenty-five, Lucinda had thrice won the Badminton Horse Trials, and twice the European Championships, and was awarded the M.B.E. in 1978. An intrepid horsewoman, Lucinda, who was born at Appleshaw, loves the countryside around her, and is content to spend her life there, although she does love to travel. She likes cross-country riding best, gruelling though it is, and says cheerfully, "I've got a lot of work to do on dressage and show-jumping."

Lucinda's favourite horse is Be Fair, a chestnut stallion with a white blaze on his soft nose, retired now, but occupying a stable near to the house. There are half a dozen horses always in the stables, with new ones coming to train.

The lanes wander around to Enham-Alamein, on the road north to Newbury. Beside a row of tall trees where rooks build their nests in spring, and behind a white flag-pole, stands the red brick St George's, the Alamein Church. It is a small place, scrupulously clean, light and airy, a memorial to the men who fought at that decisive battle in the Western Desert in 1943. Its walls are cream-washed, the wood floor polished to a shine, and all its furnishings – pews, font, lectern, pulpit and altar are in plain, smooth teak, undecorated except for discreet brass plaques and small regimental shields. Most of the windows are plain, except those in the east wall and one or two others; one is the 'Montgomery window', presented by his brother in memory of Field Marshal Viscount Montgomery of

Alamein, and incorporating the badge of the Royal Warwick-
shire Regiment.

The church is very masculine, very military, very funct-
ional; a splendid and appropriate tribute to a valiant army. but
I felt very lonely there.

A detour to the east brings us to Whitchurch, and inevitably, to the Test again. A hundred yards or so on the Winchester side of the town's main cross-roads, is the Whitchurch
Silk Mill, a business unique in Hampshire; there are only a few
such mills in the whole of the British Isles, and in England, I
think, only two others, in Suffolk and in Macclesfield. But
here, a weaving industry of some sort was recorded in the
Domesday survey.

The present eighteenth-century building, three storeys high,
with a small bell-tower above, is classified as of Architectural
and Historic Interest, and there are plans to restore the old
waterwheel to working condition. Until the 1930s, the wheel
was the only source of power for the looms, but it hasn't been
used since electricity was installed. The walls are faced with
red brick for added insulation, for the mill stands on its own
island in the river, which naturally creates a damp atmosphere,
particularly in late autumn when the mists rise from the
water. The damp has not affected the gable clock though, a
memento celebrating the victorious Battle of Waterloo in
1815, and still keeping good time.

This has always been a family business, and is so still,
employing local women who sit at their looms weaving
incredibly fine fibres, like spiders' threads. The mill deals in
other fabrics as well, but 85 per cent of its business is concerned with silk, which is imported from China in skein form,
woven at Whitchurch, and sent elsewhere to be dyed and
finished. There is a commercial shop on the premises, and
visitors are encouraged to look around.

By returning to the cross-roads and turning right Overton,
you pass on the left, the picturesque crescent of thatched
cottages at Freefolk, just before the mill where their occupants
worked. The cottages were built to house workers of the paper
mill, Portals Ltd, which has changed location several times
during its long life, first at Bere Mill, then at Laverstoke, and
since 1922 at a purpose-built complex at Overton.

Henri de Portal came to England early in the 1700s, having

been smuggled out of France to escape the persecution being suffered by Huguenots there. He was only a boy, and was apprenticed to a paper mill on the River Itchen near Southampton.

In 1711, Henri applied to Winchester Quarter Sessions to become a naturalised Englishman, and was known henceforth as Henry Portal. With the assistance of his wealthy and influential friend, William Heathcote of Hursley, he set up his own paper-making mill on the Test. Henry was a good worker and an able businessman; and he made a high-quality product. He quickly moved to larger premises at Laverstoke, and by the end of 1724 he had secured a contract with the Bank of England to make paper for bank-notes.

Portals has continued to grow ever since, and bank-note and security paper is made there not only for Great Britain, but for 125 countries all over the world. Portals of Overton are the largest producers of currency paper, with an international reputation for reliability, service and security, a unique and happy position of which Henry Portal, Huguenot refugee, would have been justly proud.

The river is quite sizeable at Overton, but only a mile or so to the east, in the tiny village of Ashe, the beautiful Test has its source; in a farm-field just visible from the road, the spring wells up from the ground, and starts its long journey, providing work and income for many, and beauty for everyone.

The Test's northernmost tributary is the pretty little Bourne rivulet, which rises beyond Hurstbourne Tarrant near Upton; since Upton is not over-far from the county's border with Wiltshire and Berkshire, the Bourne is the most northerly south-flowing river in Hampshire.

St Mary Bourne is a picture-book village, with watercress beds where moorhens potter, and sheep on the green slopes behind; a variety of cottages edge the winding main street, and the clear stream trickles through.

The church of St Mary Bourne is charming, flint-walled and low, with a square west tower. There is an effigy on the south wall of Sir Roger des Andelys, who was killed in the Crusade of 1209 against the French heretics. A wide Norman arch leads to the chancel, and on show is a 'Vinegar Bible' of 1717, open at the error which gives it the name, the printing of the word 'vinegar' instead of 'vineyard' in the parable in Luke XX.

The main treasure of the church is the font, the fourth, and largest, of the Tournai fonts in Hampshire. It is less decorated than the others, and stands on a giant, plain central trunk of polished black marble, with four smaller trunks in each corner, a fantastic piece of engineering. The other three of the seven Tournai fonts brought to England are at Lincoln, Ipswich and Thornton Curtis, in Humberside.

The A34 northwards leads straight out of the county into Berkshire, and there are not very many Hampshire miles left after Burghclere. In this village, in 1926, were built a chapel and two almshouses, in memory of Harry Willoughby Sandham, R.A.S.C., who served in France and Macedonia in the First World War.

The chapel is a small building, only about thirty by twenty feet, and quite high, with a simple altar. It is owned now by the National Trust, and although it is the Sandham Memorial, it is the spirit of Sir Stanley Spencer that the visitor remembers. For the walls are covered from floor to ceiling with Spencer paintings, and in the silence of this tiny chapel, they are a sobering experience.

Sir Stanley himself served with the Royal Berkshire Regiment in that bloodbath farcically called 'the war to end all wars', first as a hospital orderly at home, and then on the Salonica front in Greece. The murals are in oils on canvas, and took six years to execute, from 1926 to 1932. It is not a place to glance around and go away; it is a place to sit, to study, and to think.

Here, in these very personal paintings, is expressed what has been called "the impact of a world cataclysm on one gifted man". There are no gruesome scenes, no pretence of glory, no horror, no romance; there is only reality, the unutterably dreary routine of war; the daily drudgery of makeshift hospital wards, the basic hardships of setting up endlesss temporary field camps.

The great mural filling the wall behind the altar is called The Resurrection, and took nearly a year to complete. It shows soldiers handing in to the Saviour the crosses which are no longer needed to mark their graves. I find the room infinitely sad.

Outside, the hills rise high, edged with the ridge of Beacon Hill, habitat of walkers, kite-flyers and model aeroplane enthusiasts. There is something very clean about the landscape of north Hampshire; clean, and spacious, and fresh, and green, and permanent. I would like the war-mongers and spoilers of the world to contemplate a while in the Sandham Memorial, and then go out into those hills to reflect, not on what they want, but on what they have.

We in Hampshire should be especially thankful; for we have more than most.

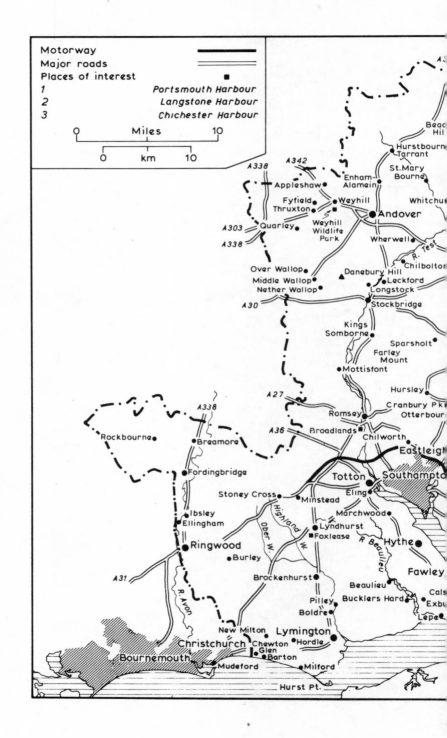

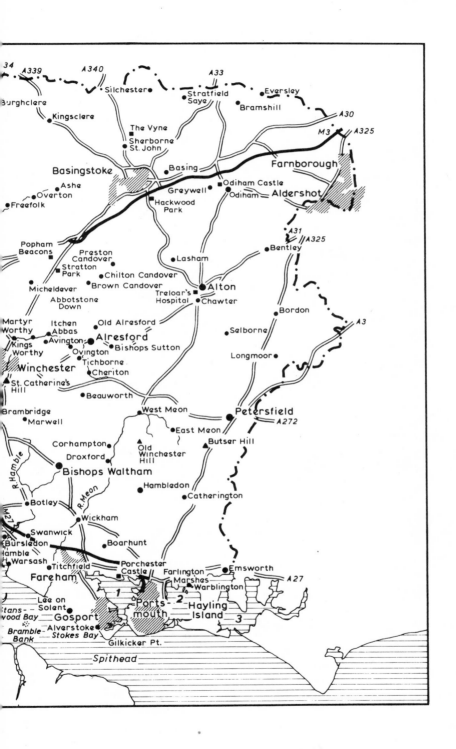

INDEX